the DINNER CREATIONS COOKBOOK

Diane Krause

Southern Road Press

www.dinnercreationscookbook.com

Second Printing, 2013

ISBN-13: 978-1490931210
ISBN-10: 149093121X

Published by Southern Road Press
Friendswood, Texas

www.dinnercreationscookbook.com

INTRODUCTION

Dinner Creations operated in Friendswood, Texas, from 2004 to 2008 and was one of the first meal assembly businesses in the Houston area.

Through the business of Dinner Creations, we gained a whole new family. We shared life stories, celebrated weddings, and rejoiced over the addition of new little ones to families. We watched people provide care and comfort to others through the gift of food and considered it a blessing to be a part of that caring. We made new friends, and we had a very good time doing the business of Dinner Creations.

This book is a collection of the recipes from Dinner Creations. Perhaps these recipes will enrich your family, and maybe even help you extend a bit of care to those around you. From all of us who have been a part of Dinner Creations, thank you for letting us have a place around your dinner table.

> --- Diane Krause
> Owner, Dinner Creations

For your convenience, printable freezer labels for all recipes in The Dinner Creations cookbook are available at: www.dinnercreationscookbook.com.

Make-Ahead and Freezer Notes

Meal assembly businesses have allowed families to prepare entrees ahead of time and stock freezers for simple, thaw-and-cook meals on busy days. All of the recipes in this collection are designed to be freezer-friendly. If freezer meals are new to you, here are a few notes to get you started.

Dinner Creations used the USDA guidelines for freezing and food safety for all freezing and thawing instructions. As of the date of this printing, the complete USDA publication can be found at: **http://www.fsis.usda.gov/Fact_Sheets/Focus_On_Freezing/index.asp.**

In general, we recommend thawing most dishes in the refrigerator for 48 hours. Two sections from the USDA guidelines are included here ("Safe Defrosting" and "Cooking Frozen Food"). More information can be found by visiting the USDA website referenced here.

Safe Defrosting

Never defrost foods in a garage, basement, car, dishwasher or plastic garbage bag; out on the kitchen counter, outdoors or on the porch. These methods can leave your foods unsafe to eat.

There are three safe ways to defrost food: in the refrigerator, in cold water, or in the microwave. It's best to plan ahead for slow, safe thawing in the refrigerator. Small items may defrost overnight; most foods require a day or two. And large items like turkeys may take longer, approximately one day for each 5 pounds of weight.

For faster defrosting, place food in a leak proof plastic bag and immerse it in cold water. (If the bag leaks, bacteria from the air or surrounding environment could be introduced into the food. Tissues can also absorb water like a sponge, resulting in a watery product.) Check the water frequently to be sure it stays cold. Change the water every 30 minutes. After thawing, cook immediately.

When microwave-defrosting food, plan to cook it immediately after thawing because some areas of the food may become warm and begin to cook during microwaving.

Cooking Frozen Foods

Raw or cooked meat, poultry or casseroles can be cooked or reheated from the frozen state. However, it will take approximately one and a half times the usual cooking time for food which has been thawed. Remember to discard any wrapping or absorbent paper from meat or poultry.

When cooking whole poultry, remove the giblet pack from the cavity as soon as you can loosen it. Cook the giblets separately. Read the label on USDA-inspected frozen meat and poultry products. Some, such as pre-stuffed whole birds, MUST be cooked from the frozen state to ensure a safely cooked product.

Table of Contents

Pork

Beef

Seafood

BREAKFAST

CRUNCHY STUFFED FRENCH TOAST
with STRAWBERRY SAUCE

Serves 8

8 ounces cream cheese, softened
1/4 cup powdered sugar

16 slices day old bread

4 eggs
2 cups milk
1 tsp. vanilla

4 cups crushed corn flakes

Strawberry Sauce:
2 cups (about 12 ounces) frozen sweetened strawberries
2 tsp. cornstarch

Preheat oven to 350°F. Spray a large cookie sheet or baking sheet with nonstick cooking spray, or line baking sheet with foil and coat with cooking spray.

With a hand mixer, beat the cream cheese with powdered sugar. Spread cream cheese filling over 8 slices of the bread; top with the remaining bread slices to make 8 sandwiches.

In a bowl, whisk together the eggs, milk and vanilla. Pour the crushed cornflakes into a shallow pan. Dip each sandwich in the milk mixture, then coat with the cornflakes, pressing to adhere. Lay each sandwich on the prepared baking sheet. Bake for 30 to 40 minutes.

Combine strawberries and cornstarch in a small saucepan. Heat over low heat, stirring frequently, until thickened. Serve over baked French toast.

FREEZER PREPARATION: Prepare sandwiches as directed, through the cornflake coating step. Lay sandwiches in a rectangular freezer container, layering with waxed paper sheets if necessary. Cover pan tightly and label. Mix strawberries and cornstarch and pour into a plastic container with tight-fitting lid, or in a one-quart freezer bag; seal and label.

CANADIAN BACON BREAKFAST STRATA

Serves 8

4 English muffins, split
8 slices (about 6 ozs.) Canadian bacon
1 1/4 cups shredded sharp Cheddar cheese
1/3 cup finely shredded Parmesan cheese

8 large eggs
3 cups milk
1 1/2 Tbsp. Dijon mustard
1/2 tsp. salt
1/4 tsp. black pepper
1/4 tsp. Tabasco

Preheat oven to 350°F. Spray a 9 x 13 baking pan with nonstick cooking spray. Arrange muffin halves, cut side down, on bottom of baking dish. Top the muffin halves with slices of Canadian bacon, then with the Cheddar and Parmesan cheeses.

In a large bowl, whisk together the eggs, milk, mustard, salt, pepper and Tabasco. Pour liquid mixture over the muffins. Let strata rest while oven is preheating.

Bake, uncovered, about 1 1/2 hours, or until strata is puffed and set in the center. (Cover loosely with foil if strata starts to brown too quickly.)

Let stand 10 minutes, then cut and serve.

FREEZER PREPARATION: Assemble strata as directed but do not bake. Cover tightly, label and freeze.

BACK-TO-SCHOOL OATMEAL BARS

Yields 24 bars

3/4 cup butter, softened
3/4 cup brown sugar
1/3 cup sugar
1 egg
1 1/2 tsp. vanilla extract
1 1/2 cups flour
1 tsp. baking soda
2 cups quick-cooking oats
3/4 cups chocolate chips, or other flavored chips
1/2 cup raisins
1/2 cup nuts, chopped (optional)

Preheat oven to 350° F. Spray a 9 x 13 baking pan with nonstick cooking spray, or line with foil.

Cream softened butter with sugars. Add egg and vanilla extract and mix well. Stir together the flour and baking soda, then add to butter mixture. Stir in oats, chips and raisins. Spread batter into prepared pan. Bake for 25-30 minutes or until golden brown. Cool in pan, then cut into bars.

FREEZER PREPARATION: Mix batter as directed and spread in pan; do not bake. Cover tightly, label and freeze.

CHRISTMAS MORNING CASSEROLE

Serves 10

8 ounces cream cheese, softened
1 cup sugar
1/2 tsp. vanilla
1 tsp. ground cinnamon
12 slices sourdough bread

10 eggs
1 cup (8 ounces) milk
1 cup (8 ounces) evaporated milk
3 ounces cream cheese, softened
1/2 cup white sugar
1/2 tsp. salt

1/4 cup (1/2 stick) butter, melted
1/2 cup chopped pecan pieces

Maple Vanilla Sauce:
3/4 cup brown sugar
3 Tbsp. maple syrup
3/4 cup (6 ounces) evaporated milk

1/4 cup + 2 Tbsp. butter
3/4 tsp. vanilla extract

Preheat oven to 350°F. Spray a 9 x 13 baking pan with nonstick cooking spray.

With a hand mixer, beat the 8 ounces cream cheese with sugar, vanilla and cinnamon until smooth. Spread mixture evenly over 6 slices of the bread. Top with remaining slices to make sandwiches. Tear or cut the sandwiches into pieces and lay pieces in prepared pan, pressing down to fit.

In a large bowl, using the same hand mixer, mix the eggs, milk, evaporated milk, 3 ounces cream cheese, sugar and salt. Slowly pour over the bread in the pan, letting the milk mixture soak in. Drizzle all with melted 1/4 cup butter and pecan pieces.

Bake, uncovered, for 1 hour or until knife inserted in center comes out clean. Serve with Maple Vanilla Sauce.

For sauce, combine brown sugar, maple syrup, evaporated milk and butter in a medium saucepan. Bring to a boil over medium heat; boil for 5 minutes, stirring often. Remove from heat and stir in vanilla extract.

FREEZER PREPARATION: Prepare casserole as directed but do not bake. Cover dish tightly, label and freeze. Handle carefully, since this dish contains a lot of liquid. Maple Vanilla Sauce may be made ahead and frozen in a plastic container with tight-fitting lid.

PASTA

BAKED SPAGHETTI BOLOGNESE

Serves 6-8

1 lb. ground beef
1 1/4 cups prepared marinara sauce
1 1/2 tsp. sugar

9 ounces angel hair pasta (cappellini)

1 1/4 cups shredded Cheddar cheese
1 1/4 cups shredded Monterey Jack cheese

Preheat oven to 375°F. Spray a 9 x 13 baking pan with nonstick cooking spray.

Cook ground beef in a large skillet until beef is cooked through and no longer pink, breaking up any large pieces. Drain the meat, then return it to the skillet and stir in the marinara sauce and sugar. Set aside.

Cook angel hair pasta according to package directions; drain pasta and rinse with cool water.

To assemble, spread 2 cups meat sauce over the bottom of the prepared baking dish. Top with half of the cooked pasta, then sprinkle over 1/2 cup Cheddar and 1/2 cup Monterey Jack cheese. Top with 2 cups meat sauce, the remaining pasta, and another 1/2 cup Cheddar and 1/2 cup Monterey Jack cheese. Cover with the remaining 2 cups meat sauce, then sprinkle over the remaining cheese.

Bake uncovered for 30-40 minutes.

FREEZER PREPARATION: Prepare casserole as directed, omitting the cheese topping. Measure last 1/4 cup of Cheddar and Monterey Jack cheeses into a plastic sandwich bag; seal. Lay a sheet of deli paper or waxed paper over casserole, then place bag of cheese on top. Seal entire pan well and label.

BAKED ZITI

Serves 8

8 oz. ground beef
1/2 cup chopped onion
4 cups marinara sauce
12 ounces Ziti pasta, cooked according to package directions
6 slices Provolone cheese
1 cup sour cream or ricotta cheese

1 1/4 cups shredded Mozzarella cheese
2 Tbsp. grated Parmesan cheese

> **Handy Tip:**
> Sour cream breaks down and becomes watery if frozen. If freezing this dish, ricotta cheese may be substituted.

Preheat oven to 350°F. Spray 9 x 13 baking pan with cooking spray; set aside.

In a large skillet, brown ground beef with chopped onion until beef is no longer pink; drain and return to skillet, turning off heat. Add marinara to the beef and mix well.

Spoon about 1/2 cup sauce over the bottom of prepared baking pan. Spread 3 cups cooked pasta over the sauce. Lay the 6 slices Provolone over the pasta. Add the sour cream or ricotta cheese and spread evenly over the Provolone. Carefully spread 2 cups of the marinara and beef sauce over the sour cream, then top with the remaining cooked pasta. Sprinkle 1 1/4 cups mozzarella over the pasta, then top with the remaining marinara and beef sauce. Sprinkle Parmesan over the top.

Bake uncovered for 30-45 minutes, or until bubbly around the edges and heated through. Let rest for at least 5 minutes before serving.

FREEZER PREPARATION: Prepare dish as directed, substituting ricotta cheese for sour cream if desired. Cover, seal and label.

PENNE PASTA with ITALIAN SAUSAGE

Serves 6

6 cups cooked penne pasta (about 8 ounces dry)

3/4 lb. Italian sausage
2 1/2 cups (about 18 ounces) prepared pasta sauce
1 cup diced tomatoes, undrained
2 cloves garlic, minced
1 Tbsp. dried parsley
1 Tbsp. brown sugar
1 tsp. Italian seasoning
1/2 tsp. oregano
1/2 tsp. black pepper

1 1/2 cups shredded Parmesan cheese
1 1/2 cups shredded Mozzarella cheese

Preheat oven to 350°F. Spray a 9 x 13 baking pan with nonstick cooking spray.

If using link sausage, remove sausage casings. Brown sausage in a skillet over medium-high heat until it is browned and loses pink color. Drain well.

In a large bowl, mix the penne pasta, cooked sausage, pasta sauce, diced tomatoes, garlic, parsley, brown sugar, Italian seasoning, oregano and pepper. In another bowl, or plastic reclosable bag, combine the two cheeses and mix well. Stir 1 3/4 cups cheese mixture into the pasta and sausage mixture.

Spoon pasta mixture into prepared baking pan. Top with remaining cheese. Bake, covered, for 30 to 40 minutes. Uncover and bake an additional 5 to 10 minutes or until cheese is melted.

FREEZER PREPARATION: Prepare casserole as directed, topping with cheese. Cover tightly (if using foil, cover food with plastic wrap before foil); label and freeze.

RAVIOLI BAKE

Serves 6

28 ounces cheese filled ravioli, refrigerated or frozen
2 1/4 cups (about 18 ounces) prepared pasta sauce
1 cup diced tomatoes, undrained
1/2 tsp. dried oregano
2 cloves garlic, minced
1/4 cup dry white wine
1 Tbsp. dried parsley
1/2 tsp. black pepper
1/2 tsp. Italian seasoning
1 1/2 cups shredded Mozzarella cheese

Preheat oven to 375°F. Spray a 9 x 13 baking pan with nonstick cooking spray.

Cook ravioli according to package directions; drain well.

In a large bowl, combine the pasta sauce, tomatoes, oregano, garlic, white wine, parsley, pepper and Italian seasoning. Gently stir in cooked ravioli. Spoon pasta mixture into prepared baking pan.

Bake pasta, uncovered, for 20 minutes. Top with Mozzarella cheese and bake an additional 10 minutes, or until cheese is melted.

FREEZER PREPARATION: Prepare casserole as directed but do not bake. Package Mozzarella cheese in a plastic bag; seal. Freeze bag of cheese separately, or lay on top of casserole, separating with a sheet of waxed

ONE-POT SPAGHETTI

Serves 6

1 lb. ground beef
3/4 cup chopped onion
1 cup sliced fresh mushrooms, optional
2 cloves garlic, minced
3 cups beef broth
2 1/4 cups water
1 6-ounce can tomato paste
1 1/2 tsp. dried oregano
2 tsp. dried basil
1/2 tsp. black pepper
10 ounces dry spaghetti
1/2 cup grated Parmesan cheese

Brown ground beef with onions in a large skillet over medium-high heat until beef loses its pink color. Drain beef and wipe out skillet. Return meat to skillet. Stir in mushrooms, garlic, beef broth, water, tomato paste, oregano, basil and black pepper. Bring to a boil. Break spaghetti into 2" to 3" pieces and add to skillet, a little at a time and stir until spaghetti is covered with liquid.

Reduce heat to medium-low and simmer, uncovered, for 17 to 20 minutes, or until spaghetti is tender.

Serve with Parmesan cheese.

FREEZER PREPARATION: Cook ground beef with onions as directed; drain and cool, then package in a one-quart freezer bag. In a one-gallon freezer bag, combine the mushrooms, garlic, broth, water, tomato paste, oregano, basil and black pepper; seal tightly (double-bag if desired). Break spaghetti into 2" to 3" pieces and package in one-quart freezer bag. Portion Parmesan in a separate bag. Combine all bags in a separate one- or two-gallon freezer bag; label and freeze.

FETTUCCINE ALFREDO with SHRIMP

Serves 6

12 ounces dry fettuccine noodles
8 ounces cream cheese, softened (can use low fat or fat free)
1/3 cup (5 1/3 Tbsp.) butter
1/2 cup skim milk
1 1/2 cups (12 ounces) low fat evaporated milk
2 cloves garlic, minced
1/2 cup (4 ounces) chicken broth
1 tsp. chicken base or chicken bouillon granules
1/2 cup grated Parmesan cheese
1/4 cup grated Romano cheese
1 pinch nutmeg
1 tsp. black pepper
2 Tbsp. olive oil
1 lb. shrimp (31-40 count), peeled and deveined
6 cloves garlic, minced
1 Tbsp. Worcestershire sauce   1/4 tsp. salt
1/2 tsp. oregano   1/2 tsp. black pepper

Cook fettuccine noodles according to package directions; drain, rinse and set aside.

Spray a large nonstick skillet with nonstick cooking spray. Heat the cream cheese and butter over medium heat and stir until butter is melted. Gently stir in the skim milk, evaporated milk, 2 cloves garlic, chicken broth and chicken base. Cook over medium heat until sauce is blended, stirring often. Stir in cheeses, nutmeg and 1 tsp. black pepper. Cook on low until sauce is thickened.

In another skillet, heat the 2 Tbsp. olive oil over medium-high heat, then add the shrimp, garlic, Worcestershire, oregano, salt and black pepper. Saute for 2 to 3 minutes or until shrimp are opaque.

Stir fettuccine noodles into Alfredo sauce; serve in bowls or on plates topped with sauteed shrimp.

FREEZER PREPARATION: Cook noodles as directed; drain, rinse and cool. Toss lightly with vegetable oil to prevent sticking. Whisk together the skim milk, evaporated milk, broth, base and 2 cloves garlic; pour into a one-gallon freezer bag and seal tightly. Wrap 8 ounces cream cheese and 1/3 cup butter in plastic wrap and package in one-quart freezer bag; seal. Mix Parmesan and Romano with nutmeg and pepper; package in a separate freezer bag. Toss shrimp with 6 cloves garlic, Worcestershire, salt and pepper; package in a one-gallon freezer bag; seal. Combine all packages into a two-gallon freezer bag; label and freeze.

POULTRY

CHICKEN NOTES

One medium to large boneless, skinless chicken breast will weigh about **6 ounces**

One **6-ounce** raw boneless, skinless chicken breast = **1 1/2 cups** diced cooked chicken

One pound raw boneless, skinless chicken breast meat = **4 cups** diced cooked chicken

One **3 lb.** whole chicken = about **4 1/2 cups** diced cooked chicken

COOKING GUIDE FOR CHICKEN

CHICKEN	WEIGHT	ROASTING 350°F	SIMMER	GRILL
Whole Broiler-Fryer	3 to 4 lbs.	1 1/4 to 1 1/2 hours	60 to 75 minutes	60 to 75 minutes
Whole Roasting Hen	5 to 7 lbs.	2 to 2 1/4 hours	1 3/4 to 2 hours	18 to 25 minutes/lb.
Whole Cornish Hen	18 to 24 ounces	50 to 60 minutes	35 to 40 minutes	45 to 55 minutes/lb.
Breast Half, bone-in	6 to 8 ounces	30 to 40 minutes	35 to 45 minutes	10 to 15 minutes/side
Breast Half, Boneless	4 ounces	20 to 30 minutes	25 to 30 minutes	6 to 8 minutes/side
Thighs	4 ounces	40 to 50 minutes	40 to 50 minutes	10 to 15 minutes/side
Drumsticks	4 ounces	35 to 45 minutes	40 to 50 minutes	8 to 12 minutes/side

TIP:

For nice, even cubes of cooked chicken breast, trim boneless, skinless chicken breasts of all visible fat and/or tendons. Cut the raw chicken into evenly-sized cubes (about 1/4"). Bring salted water to boil in a large saucepan or soup pot. Drop in the chicken pieces, stir well and remove the pan from the heat. Cover the pan and let the chicken sit for 5 to 7 minutes, then spoon out the chicken into a large bowl to cool. If using the chicken in a dish that will be baked, remove the chicken from the water after about 4 minutes. Chicken will continue cooking in the oven.

KING RANCH CHICKEN

Serves 8

1/4 cup diced onion
1/2 cup cream of chicken soup
1/2 cup cream of celery soup
1/2 cup sour cream
1/2 cup chicken broth
1 cup (8 ounces) diced tomatoes with green chiles
1 tsp. chili powder
1/2 tsp. cumin
1/2 tsp. garlic powder
1/4 tsp. black pepper
8 ounces cubed or shredded processed cheese (Velveeta or equivalent)
1 cup shredded Cheddar cheese

3 1/2 cups chopped cooked chicken
8 6" corn tortillas, cut into eighths
1/2 cup shredded Cheddar cheese

> **Handy Tip:**
>
> If you like spicy foods, go ahead and use a full 10-ounce can of tomatoes with green chiles.

Preheat oven to 350°F. Spray a 9 x 13 baking pan with nonstick cooking spray.

In a large bowl, combine the onions, soups, sour cream, chicken broth, diced tomatoes with green chiles, chili powder, cumin, garlic powder and black pepper. Stir in the cheeses, cooked chicken and tortillas. Pour mixture into prepared pan. Sprinkle 1/2 cup Cheddar cheese over top.

Bake, uncovered, for 35-45 minutes, or until heated through.

FREEZER PREPARATION: Prepare as directed but do not bake. Cover dish tightly, label and freeze.

CHICKEN POT PIE

Serves 6

1/3 cup flour
1/3 cup (5 1/3 Tbsp.) butter, melted
2 1/4 cups milk, divided

1 10.75-ounce can cream of chicken soup
1 Tbsp. chicken base, or chicken bouillon granules
1 pinch nutmeg
1 Tbsp. parsley
1/2 tsp. black pepper

1 lb. cooked chicken, chopped
1 cup diced carrot
1 cup peas
1 cup diced celery
3/4 cup potato cubes
1/2 cup chopped onion

One prepared pie crust (to fit baking dish)

> **Handy Tip:**
>
> Fresh potatoes will turn gray if frozen; therefore, if freezing this dish, fresh potatoes will need to be par-boiled for about 5 minutes before using. You can use frozen potato pieces as an alternative.

Preheat oven to 375°F. Spray a 9 x 13 baking pan with nonstick cooking spray.

In a large bowl, whisk together the flour, 1/3 cup melted butter and 1/4 cup milk until smooth. Whisk in the remaining 2 cups milk, cream of chicken soup, chicken base, nutmeg, parsley and black pepper. Stir in cooked chicken, carrots, peas, celery, potatoes and onion. Pour into prepared pan.

Roll out pie crust to fit baking dish. Carefully lay over filling, tucking in edges. Cut 3 to 6 slits in top of pie crust to allow steam to escape during baking. Bake, uncovered, for 45 minutes or until crust is browned and filling is bubbly. Let rest 5 minutes before serving.

FREEZER PREPARATION: Prepare pot pie as directed but do not bake. Cover dish tightly, label and freeze. Handle carefully -- the filling in this dish can be very messy.

CHICKEN SPAGHETTI

Serves 8

2 Tbsp. butter or margarine
1/2 cup mushrooms, chopped
1 cup diced onion

12 ounces spaghetti

1 10.75-ounce can cream of mushroom soup
2 Tbsp. flour
1 cup milk
2 Tbsp. diced pimientos
1 2.25-ounce can sliced ripe olives, drained
1/4 tsp. salt
1/4 tsp. pepper
8 ounces (½ cup) processed cheese, cubed or shredded*
1 lb. chicken breasts, cooked and diced

3/4 cup shredded Cheddar cheese

Velveeta; or can substitute shredded American cheese

Preheat oven to 350°F. Spray a 9 x 13 baking pan with nonstick cooking spray.

Saute mushrooms and onion in butter in a small skillet for 3-4 minutes; cool and set aside. Cook spaghetti according to package directions; drain, rinse and cool.

In a large bowl, mix the cream of mushroom soup, flour, milk, sauteed onions and mushrooms, pimientos, olives, salt, pepper and processed cheese. Add the cooked spaghetti and cooked chicken and mix well (mixing with your hands works best). Pour mixture into prepared pan.

Bake, uncovered, for 40 minutes. Sprinkle Cheddar cheese over the top and bake an additional 10 to 15 minutes, or until cheese is melted.

FREEZER PREPARATION: Prepare casserole as directed, without Cheddar cheese topping. Portion 3/4 cup shredded Cheddar cheese in small plastic bag; seal. Lay a small sheet of waxed paper or deli paper over casserole; lay bag of Cheddar on top. Cover casserole tightly; label and freeze.

CREAMY CHICKEN & RICE BAKE

Serves 8

2 Tbsp. butter or vegetable oil
1 cup chopped mushrooms
3/4 cup diced onions
1/2 cup diced red bell pepper

2 10.75-ounce cans cream of celery soup
2 tsp. chicken base or chicken bouillon granules
1/3 cup mayonnaise
1 1/4 cups milk
1/2 tsp. black pepper
1/2 tsp. dried marjoram
1/2 tsp. dried parsley

3/4 cup diced or shredded carrots
1 cup frozen peas

12 ounces cooked chicken breast meat, diced
4 cups cooked rice

3/4 cup French fried onions, lightly crushed

Preheat oven to 350°F. Spray a 9 x 13 baking pan with nonstick cooking spray.

In a skillet, saute the mushrooms, onions and red bell pepper in the butter or oil; set aside.

In a large bowl, mix the cream of celery soup, chicken base, mayonnaise, milk, pepper, marjoram and parsley. Stir in the sauteed vegetables, carrots, peas, cooked chicken and rice. Spread mixture into prepared pan; top with French fried onion pieces.

Bake, covered, for 30 minutes; uncover and bake an additional 15 to 20 minutes.

FREEZER PREPARATION: Prepare casserole as directed, but do not bake. Cover tightly, label and freeze.

CHICKEN D'IBERVILLE

Serves 8

3 cups chopped cooked chicken
2 Tbsp. sherry (do not use "cooking sherry")
1/3 cup sliced celery
1/2 cup chopped green onion
2 cups sliced mushrooms
1/4 tsp. curry powder
1/4 tsp. black pepper
5 cups cooked long grain and wild rice
1/2 cup (1 stick) butter, melted
1/2 cup sour cream
2 cups (about 17 ounces) cream of mushroom soup

3/4 cup crushed Ritz crackers
3/4 cup crushed French-fried onion pieces
1/4 tsp. paprika
1/4 tsp. garlic powder
1/4 cup (1/2 stick) butter, melted

Preheat oven to 350°F. Spray a 9 x 13 baking pan with nonstick cooking spray.

In a large bowl, mix together the chicken, sherry, celery, green onion, mushrooms, curry powder, black pepper, rice mixture, melted butter, sour cream and soup. Mix well and pour into prepared baking pan.

In another bowl, mix together the Ritz crackers, onion pieces, paprika, garlic powder and melted butter. Sprinkle evenly over the top of the casserole.

Bake, covered, for 40 minutes; uncover and bake an additional 10 minutes.

FREEZER PREPARATION: Prepare casserole, with topping, as directed but do not bake. Cover dish tightly, label and freeze.

SOUTHERN CHICKEN CASSEROLE

Serves 8

3 1/2 cups cooked biscuit crumbs (medium to large pieces)

3 1/2 cups chopped cooked chicken (white or dark meat)
1/3 cup shredded or matchstick carrots
1/3 cup finely chopped celery
3/4 cup finely chopped onion

4 1/2 cups chicken broth
1 tsp. chicken base or chicken bouillon granules
2 eggs or 1/2 cup liquid egg substitute
1/2 tsp. poultry seasoning
1/4 tsp. salt
1/2 tsp. black pepper

1 cup coarsely crushed saltine crackers
2 Tbsp. melted butter

Preheat oven to 375°F. Spray a 9 x 13 baking pan with nonstick cooking spray. Spread 3 1/2 cups biscuit pieces over bottom of prepared pan.

In a large bowl, mix cooked chicken, carrots, celery and onion, then spread over the biscuit pieces. In the same bowl, mix the chicken broth, chicken base, eggs, poultry seasoning, salt and pepper; pour evenly over biscuits and chicken mixture in pan.

Sprinkle with crushed saltine crackers, then drizzle melted butter over.

Bake, uncovered, for 45 to 50 minutes or until golden brown and set. Let stand 5 to 10 minutes before serving.

FREEZER PREPARATION: Prepare casserole as directed but do not bake. Cover dish tightly; label and freeze.

CHICKEN IN A POTATO BASKET

Serves 8

6 cups (about 27 ounces) frozen shredded hash bro[wn]
5 Tbsp. butter, melted
1 1/2 tsp. salt
1/4 tsp. black pepper

1/2 cup chopped onions
1 Tbsp. butter or vegetable oil
2 Tbsp. butter, melted
1/4 cup flour
2 Tbsp. chicken base or chicken bouillon granules
1 tsp. Worcestershire sauce
1/2 tsp. dried basil
1 cup milk, whole or 2%
1 cup evaporated milk
3 cups cooked chicken, diced
1 cup frozen peas, thawed

1/2 cup French fried onions

I put in individual ~~cookware~~ ramekins

Preheat oven to 375°F. Spray 9 x 13 baking pan with nonstick cooking spray.

In a large bowl, combine the hash brown potatoes, 5 Tbsp. melted butter, salt and pepper. Press mixture into prepared baking dish, covering bottom and sides (like a pie crust). Set aside.

Saute the chopped onions in 1 Tbsp. butter or oil for 3 to 4 minutes, or until translucent; set aside. Using the same large bowl (used for potato mixture), whisk together the 2 Tbsp. melted butter, flour, chicken base, Worcestershire, basil, milk and evaporated milk. Stir in sauteed onions, cooked chicken and peas. Pour into prepared potato crust, then top with French fried onions.

Bake, uncovered, for 45 to 50 minutes, or until crust is browned.

FREEZER PREPARATION: Prepare as directed but do not bake. Cover tightly and label.

BAKED CHICKEN SALAD

Serves 6

1/2 cup mayonnaise
1 10.75-ounce can cream of chicken soup
2 tsp. lemon juice
1/8 tsp. Tabasco sauce
1/4 cup sour cream
1 cup diced celery
1/4 cup pecan pieces
3 cups chopped cooked chicken

2/3 cup shredded sharp cheddar cheese
1 cup crushed potato chips

Preheat oven to 350° F. Spray an 8 x 8 baking pan with nonstick cooking spray.

In a large bowl, mix together the mayonnaise, cream of chicken soup, lemon juice, Tabasco, sour cream, celery and pecan pieces. Gently stir in the cooked chicken. Spoon into prepared pan. Top with shredded cheddar cheese and crushed potato chips.

Bake, uncovered, for 25 to 30 minutes.

FREEZER PREPARATION: Prepare as directed above but do not bake. Seal pan tightly, label and freeze.

CHICKEN ENCHILADAS

Serves 6-8

1 Tbsp. butter or vegetable oil
3/4 cup chopped onions
3 1/2 cups chicken breast meat, cooked and chopped or shredded
1 cup shredded Monterey Jack cheese, divided
1 cup shredded Cheddar cheese, divided

6 ounces cream cheese, softened
1 10.75-ounce can cream of chicken soup
1/4 tsp. salt
1/4 tsp. black pepper
1/2 cups diced green chiles
2 cloves garlic, minced
1 tsp. dried oregano
1 tsp. ground cumin
1/2 tsp. sugar
1 15-ounce chicken broth
1/2 cup salsa

8 8" flour tortillas

Preheat oven to 350°F. Spray a 9 x 13 baking dish with nonstick cooking spray.

Saute onions in butter or oil for 3 to 4 minutes, or until translucent. In a large bowl, combine the onions, cooked chicken, 1/2 cup Monterey Jack cheese and 1/2 cup Cheddar cheese.

In another large bowl, using a hand mixer, mix the softened cream cheese (if necessary, soften in a microwave until almost melted), soup, salt, pepper, green chiles, garlic, oregano, cumin, sugar, chicken broth and salsa.

On each tortilla, spread 1 to 2 Tbsp. of sauce across the tortilla, just to the side of the center, fill with chicken mixture, then roll up and place seam side down in prepared baking dish. Pour remaining sauce over the enchiladas, then top with the remaining 1/2 cup Monterey Jack and 1/2 cup Cheddar cheeses.

Bake, uncovered, for about 30 minutes, or until bubbly and cheese has melted.

FREEZER PREPARATION: Mix sauce and prepare enchiladas as directed. Do not top enchiladas with sauce and cheese (this will prevent enchiladas from becoming overly soggy). Package remaining sauce and cheese separately in freezer bags. Lay a sheet of waxed paper over enchiladas, then lay packaged sauce and cheese on top. Cover tightly and label.

CHICKEN ENCHILADAS VERDE

Serves 6-8

1 Tbsp. butter or vegetable oil
1/2 cup diced onion

3 1/2 cups chicken breast meat, cooked and chopped or shredded
2 cups shredded Monterey Jack cheese, divided
1 1/2 cups shredded Cheddar cheese, divided
1/4 cup diced green chiles
1/4 tsp. black pepper

1/2 cup chicken broth
2 1/2 cups green enchilada sauce
1/2 cup salsa verde
1/3 cup sliced or chopped black olives, optional

8 8" flour tortillas

Preheat oven to 350°F. Spray a 9 x 13 baking dish with nonstick cooking spray.

Saute onions in butter or oil for 3-4 minutes, or until translucent. In a large bowl, mix onions, chicken, 1 1/2 cup Monterey Jack cheese, 1 cup Cheddar cheese, green chiles and pepper.

In a separate bowl, mix the chicken broth and green enchilada sauce. Spread about 1/2 cup of this mixture over the bottom of prepared baking dish.

Soften tortillas for a few seconds in a microwave, if necessary, to make them pliable for rolling. Fill each tortilla with 1 Tbsp. green enchilada sauce mixture and 1/2 to 3/4 cup of the chicken filling. Roll up and place seam side down in prepared pan. Pour remaining green enchilada sauce mixture over enchiladas, then top with the salsa verde and the black olives. Sprinkle enchiladas with the remaining Monterey Jack and Cheddar cheeses.

Bake, uncovered, for 30 minutes, or until cheese is melted and enchiladas are heated through. Serve with sour cream.

FREEZER PREPARATION: Prepare as directed , but do not top the enchiladas with the green enchilada sauce mixture, salsa verde, olives and cheese. (Adding the sauce before cooking will keep enchiladas from becoming overly soggy.) Package the sauce, salsa verde, olives and cheese separately in freezer bags. Place a piece of waxed paper over enchiladas, then lay packages over the top. Cover tightly and label.

SANTA FE CHICKEN & BLACK BEANS

Serves 6

1 1/2 lbs. boneless, skinless chicken breasts, trimmed
1 15-ounce can black beans, drained and rinsed
1 3/4 cups corn
1 3/4 cups salsa, any kind
6 ounces cream cheese

> **Handy Tip:**
>
> If cooking fewer than 6 servings, adjust cooking time and monitor slow cooker often. Food may dry out or overcook if slow cooker is not full, or does not contain enough liquid.

Spray a slow cooker with nonstick cooking spray. Place chicken breasts in slow cooker. Add black beans, corn and salsa; stir gently to mix vegetables with salsa. Cover and cook on HIGH for 4 to 5 hours or LOW for 8 to 10 hours. (Can also be baked in oven for 1 to 1 1/2 hours.)

About 30 minutes before serving, drop in the cream cheese and be sure temperature is on LOW. When ready to serve, stir to blend cream cheese.

FREEZER PREPARATION: Package chicken breasts in a one-gallon freezer bag; seal. Mix beans, corn and salsa in another one-gallon freezer bag; seal. Wrap cream cheese in plastic wrap. Combine all packages in a one-gallon freezer bag; seal, label and freeze.

JALAPENO-STUFFED CHICKEN BREASTS

Serves 6

6   6-ounce boneless, skinless chicken breasts, trimmed

1 egg
1 Tbsp. water
1/4 cup packaged cornbread mix
1/2 cup flour
1/4 tsp. black pepper
1/4 tsp. cayenne pepper

12 jalapeno pepper strips (about 3 ounces canned jalapeno halves)
6 slices Monterey Jack cheese, cut in half
2 Tbsp. melted butter

Purchased salsa verde

Preheat oven to 375°F. Spray a 9 x 13 baking pan with nonstick cooking spray, or line dish with foil and coat foil with cooking spray.

In a medium bowl, beat the egg with 1 Tbsp. water; set aside. In a shallow pan, mix together the cornbread mix, flour and peppers.

Trim chicken breasts well. Lay breast on cutting board or flat surface. Holding sharp knife parallel to chicken and beginning on thicker side of breast, cut a pocket in the chicken breast, making the cut wide enough to accommodate jalapeno strip and cheese slice. Stuff each chicken breast with one piece of cheese and 2 jalapeno strips.

Holding the chicken breasts securely, dip each breast into the egg wash, then dredge in dry mixture to coat evenly. Lay breasts in prepared baking pan. Drizzle with melted butter.

Bake, uncovered, for about 45 minutes. Serve with salsa verde.

FREEZER PREPARATION: Prepare as directed but do not bake. Cover dish tightly, label and freeze.

GOAT CHEESE STUFFED CHICKEN BREASTS

Serves 6

6 6-ounce boneless, skinless chicken breasts
5 ounces goat cheese
2 Tbsp. unsalted butter, softened
2 tsp. minced fresh chives
1 1/2 tsp. minced fresh parsley
1 tsp. dried thyme
1/2 tsp. lemon juice
1 clove garlic, minced
1/4 tsp. salt
1/4 tsp. black pepper

1 egg
2 Tbsp. water

1 cup flour
2/3 cup breadcrumbs
1 Tbsp. Emeril's Essence seasoning mixture
2 Tbsp. butter, cut into 6 pieces

Preheat oven to 350°F. Spray a 9 x 13 baking dish with nonstick cooking spray.

Trim chicken breasts well. Lay breast on cutting board or flat surface. Holding sharp knife parallel to chicken and beginning on thicker side of breast, cut a pocket in the chicken breast, making the cut wide enough to accommodate cheese filling.

In a small bowl, mix the goat cheese, butter, chives, parsley, thyme, lemon juice, garlic, salt and pepper. Divide cheese mixture into 6 pieces. Put one cheese portion into the pocket of each chicken breast. In another small bowl, whisk the egg and water. In a shallow dish, combine the flour, breadcrumbs and Emeril's Essence seasoning. Dip each chicken breast in the milk mixture, then roll in the flour mixture to coat. Lay chicken breasts in prepared baking dish and top each with a pat of butter.

Bake, uncovered, for 35 to 45 minutes.

FREEZER PREPARATION: Prepare chicken breasts as directed but do not bake. Cover dish tightly, label and freeze.

CHICKEN CORDON BLEU

Serves 6

6 6-ounce boneless, skinless chicken breasts
3 thin slices ham, cut in half
3 slices Swiss cheese, cut in half

1 egg
1/2 cup milk
3/4 cup plain breadcrumbs
1/4 cup grated Parmesan cheese
2 Tbsp. dried parsley flakes

Sauce:
1 tsp. butter or margarine
1 cup sliced mushrooms
1 10.75-ounce can cream of mushroom soup
1/2 cup milk
1/2 cup chicken broth
2 tsp. Dijon mustard
2 slices Swiss cheese

Preheat oven to 350°F. Spray a 9 x 13 baking pan with nonstick cooking spray.

Trim chicken breasts well. Lay breast on cutting board or flat surface. Holding sharp knife parallel to chicken and beginning on thicker side of breast, cut a pocket in the chicken breast, making the cut wide enough to accommodate one ham and cheese slice. Insert one piece (half of a slice) of ham and one piece (half of a slice) of Swiss cheese in each pocket.

In a medium bowl, beat the egg with the 1/2 cup milk. In a shallow dish, combine the breadcrumbs, Parmesan and parsley flakes. Holding the cut side of the chicken securely, dip each chicken piece in the milk mixture, then roll in the breadrumb mixture to coat, and place in pan.

Bake, uncovered, for 40 to 45 minutes.

For sauce, saute mushrooms in butter for 3-4 minutes. Add remaining ingredients, mix well and heat on medium-low heat until cheese melts. Serve over chicken.

FREEZER PREPARATION: Prepare chicken as directed up to baking step (do not bake). For sauce, saute mushrooms in butter, then mix with soup, milk, broth and mustard. Pour into one-quart freezer bag and add the Swiss cheese. Seal tightly. Cover chicken breasts with a piece of waxed paper, then lay the bag of sauce on top. Cover pan, seal tightly and label.

CHICKEN TENDERS "ON THE RITZ"

Serves 6

1/2 cup prepared Ranch dressing (can use low-fat)
1/4 cup milk
1/2 tsp. black pepper

1 cup finely crushed Ritz crackers
1/2 cup plain breadcrumbs
2 tsp. dried parsley

16 (about 1.75 lbs.) chicken tenders

3 Tbsp. melted butter

Your choice of prepared dipping sauces (Ranch, Honey Mustard, BBQ)

Preheat oven to 375°F. Spray a baking sheet with nonstick cooking spray, or, for easier clean-up, line the cookie sheet with foil and spray foil with nonstick spray.

In a small bowl, mix the Ranch dressing, milk and pepper; set aside. In a shallow pan or dish, combine the cracker crumbs, breadcrumbs and parsley.

Dip each chicken tender into the dressing mixture, then roll in cracker crumb mixture to coat. Place tenders on prepared baking sheet, then drizzle with melted butter.

Bake, uncovered, for 10 minutes. Turn tenders over and bake an additional 10 minutes. If extra browning is desired, broil for 3 to 4 minutes. Remove from oven and serve with your choice of dipping sauces.

FREEZER PREPARATION: Prepare tenders as directed, but do not bake (can drizzle tenders with butter prior to freezing, or save this step until just before baking). Cover tightly, label and freeze.

PECAN CRUSTED CHICKEN

Serves 4 to 6

1 cup buttermilk
3 Tbsp. Emeril's Original Essence seasoning
2 tsp. salt
2 Tbsp. olive oil

3 bone-in chicken breasts, with skin
3 chicken drumsticks

1 cup finely chopped pecan pieces (preferably toasted)
1 1/4 cups all purpose flour
1/2 tsp. black pepper

Preheat oven to 400°F. Spray a baking pan liberally with nonstick cooking spray.

Whisk together buttermilk, Emeril's Essence seasoning, salt and olive oil; pour over chicken pieces in a large bowl, or a one-gallon reclosable plastic bag. Let chicken marinate 30 minutes in refrigerator.

Combine the pecan pieces, flour and pepper in a one-gallon reclosable bag. Remove chicken pieces, one or two at a time, from the buttermilk marinade and add to the bag of dry ingredients. Hold bag closed and toss chicken to coat evenly. Repeat until all chicken pieces are breaded. Lay chicken pieces, skin side down, in a single layer in prepared baking dish.

Bake, uncovered, for 25 to 30 minutes; gently turn over, skin side up, and continue baking for an additional 20 to 25 minutes or until chicken is cooked through.

FREEZER PREPARATION: Mix buttermilk marinade as directed and pour over chicken pieces in one-gallon freezer bag; seal tightly. Mix dry ingredients and package in one-gallon freezer bag; seal tightly. Place both bags in a one- or two-gallon freezer bag; seal and label.

SOUTHWESTERN OVEN-FRIED CHICKEN

Serves 6

4 1/2 cups medium breadcrumbs (Japanese breadcrumbs, or Panko, preferable)
3 Tbsp. chopped cilantro
3 Tbsp. yellow cornmeal
3 cloves garlic, minced
2 tsp. cumin
3/4 tsp. oregano
1/2 tsp. salt
1/2 tsp. cayenne pepper
1/4 tsp. ground cloves

3 Tbsp. Dijon or spicy brown mustard
1 Tbsp. water
1 1/2 Tbsp. honey

3 bone-in chicken breasts, about 6 ounces each
3 chicken drumsticks
3 chicken thighs

Preheat oven to 400°F. Spray a baking sheet or 9 x 13 baking pan with nonstick cooking spray, or line pan with foil and spray foil with cooking spray.

In a large bowl, toss the breadcrumbs with the cilantro, cornmeal, garlic, cumin, oregano, salt, cayenne pepper and cloves. In a medium bowl, mix the mustard, water and honey.

Brush chicken pieces with mustard-honey mixture, then dredge pieces in breadcrumb mixture, pressing gently to make sure crumbs adhere, then place chicken in prepared dish.

Bake, uncovered, for 45 minutes, or until chicken is crisp and brown.

FREEZER PREPARATION: Prepare chicken as directed, but do not cook. Cover dish tightly; label and freeze.

CRISPY ORANGE-SESAME CHICKEN

Serves 6

2 tsp. grated orange peel
1/2 cup orange marmalade
1/4 cup honey
2 Tbsp. Lite soy sauce
1 Tbsp. vegetable oil
1/2 tsp. sesame oil
1 tsp. hot chili sauce
1/2 tsp. salt

2 cups Japanese breadcrumbs (Panko)
1/4 to 1/2 cup sesame seeds

6 boneless, skinless chicken breasts, trimmed of any visible fat

6 fresh orange slices

Handy Tip:

For a crispy coating overall, lay the chicken breasts on a wire rack, such as a cookie cooling rack, to bake. Put the wire rack on top of the foil; spray with nonstick cooking spray, then place chicken directly on the rack. This allows even baking on all sides of the chicken.

Preheat oven to 400°F. Line a baking sheet or cookie sheet with foil and spray with nonstick cooking spray.

In a medium bowl, whisk together the orange peel, marmalade, honey, soy sauce, oils, chili sauce and salt. In another shallow pan, combine the breadcrumbs and sesame seeds.

Dip each chicken breast in the marmalade mixture, coating well, then roll in breadcrumbs, pressing to coat. Lay chicken pieces on prepared baking sheet. Dip each orange slice in marmalade mixture, then lay on top of each of the 6 chicken breasts.

Bake, uncovered, for about 20 minutes, or until chicken is firm to the touch and orange slices are lightly browned. (Cover chicken loosely with foil if coating begins to brown too quickly.)

FREEZER PREPARATION: Prepare chicken breasts as directed but do not bake. Lay in a single layer in freezer-safe dish; cover tightly, label and freeze.

CHICKEN MIRABELLA

Serves 6

6 chicken breasts (boneless or bone-in), or combination of breasts and drumsticks

1/2 cup (about 2 ounces) pitted prunes
1/2 cup pimiento-stuffed olives
2 Tbsp. capers
2 cloves garlic, crushed
1 Tbsp. dried oregano
2 tsp. salt
1 1/2 tsp. black pepper
2 bay leaves
1/3 cup red wine vinegar
3/4 cup dry white wine
1/3 cup olive oil

3/4 cup brown sugar
3 Tbsp. dried parsley flakes

Preheat oven to 350°F. Spray 9 x 13 baking pan with nonstick cooking spray or line with foil.

Trim chicken pieces, if necessary, and lay in prepared baking dish. In a medium bowl, combine prunes and next 10 ingredients. Pour over chicken. (Chicken and sauce can be made ahead and marinated before baking.) Sprinkle chicken pieces with brown sugar.

Bake, uncovered, 45 minutes for boneless, skinless chicken breasts, and up to 1 hour for bone-in pieces. Chicken should be tender and reach an internal temperature of 185°F.

Sprinkle parsley over chicken and serve.

FREEZER PREPARATION: Trim chicken pieces if necessary and place in one-gallon freezer bag. Mix sauce ingredients as directed (do not include brown sugar or parsley in sauce) and pour into bag with chicken; seal tightly. Mix brown sugar and parsley together and package in small deli cup or plastic bag; seal. Place all bags/containers in a one- or two-gallon freezer bag; seal and label.

BAKED CHICKEN in ORANGE SAUCE

Serves 6

6 boneless, skinless, chicken breasts, trimmed of any visible fat
1/2 tsp. garlic salt

1/2 cup orange marmalade
1/4 cup bottled steak sauce
1/2 cup ketchup

3 Tbsp. sliced almonds

Preheat oven to 350° F. Spray a 9 x 13 baking dish with nonstick spray, or line with foil.

Trim chicken breasts, if necessary, then lay in prepared baking pan. Sprinkle the 1/2 tsp. garlic salt over the chicken breasts (can add salt and pepper, if desired).

In a small bowl, combine the orange marmalade, steak sauce and ketchup and mix well. Pour sauce over chicken breasts. Sprinkle the almonds evenly over the chicken.

Bake in preheated oven for 40-45 minutes, or until chicken is tender and reaches an internal temperature of 165° F.

FREEZER PREPARATION: Trim chicken breasts, season with garlic salt (1/2 tsp. for 6 pieces) and lay into freezer pan, or put into one-gallon plastic freezer bag (seal bag). In a small bowl, mix together the orange marmalade, steak sauce and ketchup. Pour into a one-quart freezer bag and seal. If storing chicken in a pan or dish, lay a piece of waxed paper or plastic wrap over the chicken, then lay the bag of sauce on top. Seal dish tightly with foil and label. If storing chicken and sauce in freezer bags, place both bags into a one-gallon plastic freezer bag, seal and label.

CHICKEN in RASPBERRY-CHIPOTLE SAUCE

Serves 6

1/2 cup finely diced onion
2 cloves garlic, minced
1 Tbsp. dried chipotle flakes
1/2 cup raspberry preserves
1/2 cup frozen raspberries, thawed and mashed
1/2 cup frozen pineapple juice concentrate
1/4 cup light soy sauce
1/4 cup rice wine vinegar

6 boneless, skinless chicken breasts or bone-in chicken breasts

Preheat oven to 350°F. Spray a 9 x 13 baking dish with nonstick cooking spray, or line with foil.

Trim chicken breasts, if necessary. Lay chicken in baking dish and season with salt and pepper, if desired.

In a medium bowl, mix the diced onion, garlic, chipotle flakes, raspberry preserves, mashed raspberries, pineapple juice concentrate, soy sauce and vinegar. Pour sauce over chicken.

Bake, covered for 30 minutes. Uncover and continue baking for 10 to 15 additional minutes, or until chicken is tender (if using bone-in breasts, allow additional time).

FREEZER PREPARATION: Trim chicken breasts, if necessary. Package in one-gallon freezer bag; seal. Mix all sauce ingredients as directed and pour into a one-quart freezer bag; seal tightly. Place both bags into a one-gallon freezer bag; seal and label.

HONEY-BALSAMIC BAKED CHICKEN

Serves 6

1.5 to 2 lbs. boneless, skinless chicken breast pieces or chicken tenders

1 1/2 cups red bell pepper pieces, about 2" square
1 1/2 cups yellow or green bell pepper pieces, about 2" square
3 cups sliced mushrooms
1 14.5-ounce can diced tomatoes, undrained
3 Tbsp. olive oil
2 Tbsp. balsamic vinegar
1 Tbsp. dried rosemary
1 tsp. salt
1/2 tsp. black pepper
2 tsp. honey

Heat oven to 375°F. Spray a 9 x 13 baking pan with nonstick cooking spray.

Place chicken pieces in prepared pan. In a large bowl, mix all remaining ingredients, then pour over chicken. Bake, uncovered, for 40 to 50 minutes, or until chicken is tender.

FREEZER PREPARATION: Place chicken pieces in one-gallon freezer bag. Mix all remaining ingredients and add to chicken. Seal tightly, label and freeze.

BOSTON BEACH JERK CHICKEN

Serves 6

2 lbs. boneless, skinless chicken breast pieces or chicken tenders

1/3 cup red wine vinegar
1/3 cup soy sauce
1/4 cup brown sugar
2 tsp. thyme
1 tsp. sesame oil
2 cloves garlic, minced
1 cup diced onion
1 tsp. allspice
1 Tbsp. chopped jalapeno peppers, fresh or canned
1 Tbsp. olive oil

Place chicken pieces in a one-gallon resealable plastic bag or shallow non-metal dish.

In large bowl, mix remaining ingredients. Pour 1 cup marinade over chicken pieces. Marinate 30 minutes or up to 24 hours. Cover remaining marinade and refrigerate.

Preheat grill to medium-high heat. Remove chicken from marinade and discard marinade in bag. Place chicken on grill and cook appropriate time -- 6 to 8 minutes per side for boneless, skinless breasts, and up to 30 to 40 minutes for bone-in pieces.

Heat reserved marinade and use to baste chicken during cooking and for serving over cooked pieces.

FREEZER PREPARATION: Place chicken pieces in one-gallon freezer bag. Mix marinade and pour 1 cup marinade over chicken in bag. Package remaining marinade in plastic container with tight-fitting lid, or in a one-quart freezer bag. Place both bags into a one-gallon freezer bag; seal and label.

COUNTRY CAPTAIN CHICKEN

Serves 6

2 Tbsp. vegetable oil
1 1/2 lbs. boneless, skinless chicken breasts, cut into 3"-4" pieces
1 cup diced onion
1 bay leaf
1 tsp. curry powder
1/2 tsp. dried thyme
1/4 tsp. crushed red pepper
2 cloves garlic, minced

1 28-oz. can crushed tomatoes with juice
1 cup chicken broth
1 Tbsp. brown sugar
1/4 cup dried currants

1/4 cup slivered almonds, toasted

In a large skillet, heat vegetable oil over medium-high heat. Add chicken pieces and onion and saute for a few minutes, or until onions begin to soften. Add bay leaf, curry powder, thyme, red pepper and garlic and saute for 1 minute more. Add the tomatoes, chicken broth and brown sugar; reduce heat to medium-low and simmer for 50 to 60 minutes (reduce heat further if mixture begins to boil).

Stir in currants and cook for an additional 5 minutes. To serve, garnish with almonds.

FREEZER PREPARATION: Prepare chicken and package in a one-quart freezer bag; seal. Combine onion, bay leaf, curry powder, thyme, red pepper and garlic in another one-quart freezer bag; seal tightly. Mix together the tomatoes, chicken broth and brown sugar; package in a one-gallon freezer bag and seal tightly (double bag if desired). Portion currants and almonds each in separate small bags. Place all bags together in a two-gallon freezer bag; seal and label.

AUTUMN CHICKEN with DIJON-CIDER SAUCE

Serves 6

3/4 cup milk
2 Tbsp. cornstarch
1 Tbsp. Dijon mustard
1/8 tsp. salt
1/8 tsp. black pepper
1 pinch ground red pepper (cayenne)
1/4 cup apple cider

2 Tbsp. butter
2 cups apple slices (any variety)

1/3 cup flour
3/4 tsp. salt
1/2 tsp. black pepper

6 boneless, skinless chicken breasts (4-6 ounces each)

In a medium saucepan, whisk together the milk, cornstarch, Dijon mustard, 1/8 tsp. salt and 1/8 tsp. black pepper and cayenne pepper. Cook and stir over medium heat until begins to thicken, 3-5 minutes. Stir in the apple cider, and cook an additional 2-3 minutes. Set aside.

Melt butter in a skillet; add apples and cook over medium-high heat until tender, about 4-6 minutes. Transfer apples to an ovensafe dish and keep warm.

Mix together the flour, 3/4 tsp. salt and 1/2 tsp. black pepper in a shallow dish. Dredge chicken pieces in flour mixture to coat; add to skillet and saute over medium-high heat until cooked through, about 4 minutes per side.

To serve, place chicken breast on plate; top with apples, then spoon sauce over.

FREEZER PREPARATION: Whisk together the milk, cornstarch, Dijon mustard, salt, black pepper and ground red pepper. Pour into one-quart freezer bag or deli container with lid; seal. Combine flour, 3/4 tsp. salt and 1/2 tsp. black pepper in a one-quart freezer bag; seal. Put chicken breasts in one-gallon freezer bag; seal. Put apple slices into a one-quart freezer bag; seal. Measure apple cider into a small deli container with tight-fitting lid; seal. Measure out the 2 Tbsp. butter and wrap in plastic wrap or foil. Put all bags/containers in a large, 2-gallon freezer bag: 1 bag sauce mix; 1 bag flour mixture; 1 bag chicken breasts; 1 bag apple slices; 1 container apple cider; butter.

CHICKEN ITALIANA

Serves 6-8

1 1/2 lbs. boneless, skinless chicken breasts, trimmed and cut into large pieces

2 medium onions, peeled and quartered
1 1/2 cups sliced mushrooms
1 14.5-ounce can diced tomatoes, undrained
2 cups bottled Italian salad dressing (can use Lite or low-fat)
1 cup water
1/4 cup (.5 ounces) dry onion soup mix
2 bay leaves

Preheat oven to 375°F. Spray a 9 x 13 baking dish with nonstick cooking spray.

Lay chicken pieces in baking dish. Add onion quarters and sliced mushrooms.

In a large bowl, combine all remaining ingredients. Stir well to mix in dry soup mix, then pour over chicken pieces.

Bake, covered, for 45 to 50 minutes, or until chicken is tender. Serve stand-alone, or over rice or noodles.

FREEZER PREPARATION: Package chicken pieces in a one-gallon freezer bag with onion quarters and mushrooms; seal tightly. Mix remaining ingredients as directed and pour into one-gallon freezer bag; seal tightly. Place both bags into a one- or two-gallon freezer bag; seal and label.

CHICKEN CACCIATORE

Serves 6

1 1/2 lbs. (24 ounces) boneless, skinless, chicken breast pieces
1 cup onion slices

2 cups prepared marinara sauce
1 14.5-ounce can diced tomatoes, undrained
1/4 cup dry white wine
1 1/2 cups chicken broth
1/2 cup Italian salad dressing
2 cloves garlic, minced
1 tsp. chicken base or 1 bouillon cube
1 Tbsp. dried parsley (or 2 tsp. fresh)
1/2 tsp. dried basil
1 tsp. dried oregano
1/2 tsp. salt
1 tsp. sugar
1/2 tsp. black pepper
1 bay leaf
1 cup green bell pepper strips
1 1/2 cups sliced mushrooms

8 ounces spaghetti (capellini or spaghetti), cooked according to package directions
1/2 cup (2 ozs.) grated Parmesan cheese

SLOW COOKER METHOD: Spray slow cooker with nonstick cooking spray. Place chicken and onion slices in slow cooker. Combine next 16 ingredients and pour over chicken and onions. Cook on LOW for 4 to 5 hours. Serve over cooked pasta, topping with Parmesan cheese.

STOVETOP METHOD: Saute chicken pieces and onions in 2 Tbsp. oil in a skillet over medium-high heat. Add next 16 ingredients. Simmer over low heat for 45 to 60 minutes, or until chicken is tender. Serve over cooked pasta, topping with Parmesan cheese.

FREEZER PREPARATION: Package chicken pieces and onions in a one-gallon freezer bag; seal. Combine next 16 ingredients and pour into a one-gallon freezer bag; seal tightly. Cook pasta; drain, rinse and cool. Toss pasta with a small amount of oil to prevent sticking. Package pasta in a one-gallon freezer bag; seal. Portion Parmesan cheese in a small plastic deli cup, or in a small plastic bag. Combine all packages in a two-gallon freezer bag; seal and label.

CHICKEN CAKES with CREOLE SAUCE

Serves 6

1/4 cup finely diced red bell pepper
1/4 cup finely chopped green onions
3 cups finely chopped cooked chicken breast meat (food processor works best)
1 egg
2 Tbsp. mayonnaise
1 Tbsp. Creole mustard
1 tsp. Creole seasoning

1 cup fine, dry breadcrumbs
1 Tbsp. grated Parmesan cheese
1 Tbsp. vegetable oil

1/2 cup mayonnaise
1/4 cup plain nonfat yogurt (unsweetened)
1 1/2 tsp. minced green onion
1 clove garlic, minced
1 Tbsp. Creole mustard
1 1/2 tsp. parsley flakes
1/8 tsp. ground red pepper (cayenne)
1/8 tsp. Creole seasoning

In a large bowl, stir together the red bell pepper, green onion, chicken, egg, 2 Tbsp. mayonnaise, 1 Tbsp. Creole mustard and 1 tsp. Creole seasoning. Mix well and form into 6 patties.

Mix breadcrumbs and Parmesan in a shallow pan. Lightly roll chicken cakes in breadcrumbs and set aside.

Heat oil in a nonstick skillet over medium-high heat. Carefully saute chicken cakes for 4 to 6 minutes, or until browned on each side.

For Creole sauce, whisk together 1/2 cup mayonnaise and remaining 7 ingredients. Serve over cooked chicken cakes.

FREEZER PREPARATION: Prepare chicken cakes as directed but do not cook. Lay in freezer-safe dish, separating any layers with waxed paper. Prepare sauce as directed and package in a one-quart freezer bag. Lay a sheet over waxed paper over the top of the cakes; lay sauce packet on top. Seal, label and freeze.

BARBECUE CHICKEN PIZZA

Serves 6

3 9-inch pre-baked pizza crusts, all packaging removed

1 cup hickory smoke flavor barbecue sauce
3 tsp. honey
8 ounces (about 1 1/2 cups) chicken fajita meat, grilled and sliced
1 cup red onion slices
1 3/4 cups shredded Gouda chese
1 3/4 cups shredded Mozzarella cheese

Preheat oven to 400°F.

Place pizza crusts on baking sheet (line with foil if desired). Top each crust with:

    1/3 cup barbecue sauce
    1 tsp. honey
    1/3 cup each Gouda and Mozzarella
    1/3 of the grilled chicken pieces
    1/3 cup red onion slices
    1/4 cup each Gouda and Mozzarella

Bake pizzas 15 to 20 minutes, or until cheese is melted and pizzas are heated through.

FREEZER PREPARATION: Prepare pizzas as directed. Wrap each pizza with plastic wrap, then with foil. Seal tightly and label.

BAKED CHICKEN CHIMICHANGAS

Yields 6

2 1/4 cups cooked chicken, shredded
3/4 cup Queso Fresco or Monterey Jack cheese, shredded
3 Tbsp. chopped green onions
1 tsp. oregano
1/4 tsp. cumin
1 clove garlic, minced (or 1 tsp. prepared chopped garlic)
3 Tbsp. diced green chiles
1 1/2 cups refried beans
6 Tbsp. salsa verde

6 8" flour tortillas

Preheat oven to 375° F. Prepare a baking sheet by lining with foil or parchment paper.
(If using foil, spray the foil with nonstick cooking spray.)

In a large bowl, combine the cooked chicken, cheese, green onions, oregano, cumin, garlic and green chiles.

Before assembling chimichangas, warm the flour tortillas in an oven, microwave, or heated skillet so they are pliable for folding and rolling.

To assemble, place a tortilla on a sheet of deli paper or waxed paper. Spread 1/4 cup refried beans down the center of the tortilla, stopping about 1/2" from edge. Top with 1/2 cup chicken mixture and 1 Tbsp. salsa verde. Fold in the short sides of the tortilla, then roll up the tortilla to close.

Place chimichangas on prepared baking sheet and bake for 12-15 minutes, or until lightly browned. Serve with additional salsa verde.

FREEZER PREPARATION: Prepare chimichangas as directed. After rolling, wrap the deli paper or waxed paper tightly around the chimichanga, then twist each end to seal (like a piece of candy). Place wrapped chimichangas in a freezer bag; seal and label.

BUSH'S BBQ CHICKEN

Serves 6

3 6-ounce chicken breasts (bone-in, or boneless, skinless)
3 chicken thighs
3 chicken drumsticks

Marinade:
3 Tbsp. lemon juice
1 Tbsp. vegetable oil
1 tsp. salt
1/2 tsp. black pepper
1 clove garlic, minced

BBQ Sauce:

2 1/2 cups water
2 1/2 cups ketchup
1/4 cup apple cider vinegar
6 Tbsp. lemon juice
1 cup chopped onions

1/2 cup sugar
1/2 cup (4 ozs.) butter
1/3 cup prepared yellow mustard
1/2 tsp. black pepper
1/2 tsp. ground red pepper (cayenne)

Place chicken pieces in one-gallon resealable plastic bag, or nonmetal dish. Mix all marinade ingredients together and pour over chicken. Seal or cover, and marinate in refrigerator for 30 minutes, or up to 24 hours.

In a large bowl, combine all BBQ Sauce ingredients together and mix thoroughly.

Preheat oven to 375°F. Line a baking pan (with sides) with foil. Remove chicken from marinade and place on baking sheet. Bake, uncovered, for 30 minutes, basting with BBQ Sauce. Before baking time is up, preheat grill to medium-high heat. After baking for 30 minutes, remove chicken from oven and place on preheated grill. Cook an additional 15 to 20 minutes, turning and basting with additional BBQ sauce. (Use foil under the chicken to prevent burning the sauce.) Chicken should reach an internal temperature of 165°F. Serve with BBQ sauce.

FREEZER PREPARATION: Prepare chicken pieces and marinade as directed, packaging in a one-gallon freezer bag. Mix BBQ sauce as directed and pour into plastic deli container with tight-fitting lid, or one-quart freezer bag. Seal tightly. Package marinated chicken and BBQ Sauce in a one- or two-gallon freezer bag; seal and label.

CORNISH HENS RICARDO

Serves 4

4 Rock Cornish game hens, about 9 ounces each (have butcher butterfly, if desired)
Olive oil
Salt and pepper

4 cloves garlic, minced
1 Tbsp. dried rosemary
1 Tbsp. dried parsley
1 Tbsp. white wine
1 1/2 tsp. olive oil

1/4 cup white wine

Preheat oven to 400°F. Spray a 9 x 13 baking dish with nonstick cooking spray, or line with foil and coat with cooking spray.

Rinse game hens, place in baking pan and drizzle with a small amount of olive oil. Sprinkle with salt and pepper.

In a small bowl, mix the garlic, rosemary, parsley, 1 Tbsp. white wine and 1 1/2 tsp. olive oil. Spread this herb mixture over the top of each game hen. Pour the 1/4 cup white wine in the pan around the hens.

Roast, uncovered, for 40 to 45 minutes, tenting with foil if hens begin to brown too quickly.

FREEZER PREPARATION: Prepare as directed, but do not bake. If desired, the 1/4 cup white wine may be packaged in a separate container and added just before baking. Cover pan tightly, label and freeze.

SAN FRANCISCO ROAST CHICKEN

Serves 4

1 whole roasting chicken, about 3 pounds

3 Tbsp. soy sauce
1 tsp. brown sugar
1/4 tsp. coriander
1/2 tsp. cayenne pepper

1 lime, cut into quarters
1 clove garlic, peeled
1/2 cup onion quarters

Unwrap chicken, remove giblets (if necessary), and rinse well.

In a small bowl, mix the soy sauce, brown sugar, coriander and cayenne pepper.

Place chicken on a cutting board or in a large bowl. Drop 2 lime quarters (save remaining pieces for another use), garlic clove and onion quarters into the cavity of the chicken.

Rub the soy sauce mixture over the outside of the chicken, and place chicken in cooking dish. Pour remaining liquid over the chicken, under the skin.

Slow Cooker Method: Spray slow cooker with nonstick cooking spray. Form a piece of aluminum foil into a wad, and place in bottom of slow cooker. Place the chicken on the foil. Pour remaining soy sauce mixture over chicken, as directed. Cook on LOW for 8 to 10 hours, or on HIGH for 4 to 5 hours.

Oven Roasting Method: Spray a roasting pan with nonstick cooking spray. Preheat oven to 375°F. Roast chicken, uncovered, for 1 to 1 1/4 hours or until meat thermometer registers 165°F. Cover and let stand 10 minutes before carving.

FREEZER PREPARATION: Prepare chicken as directed but do not cook. Package in one- or two-gallon freezer bag and pour extra soy sauce mixture over. Seal tightly and label.

MANGO ROASTED CHICKEN

Serves 6

One 3 1/4 lb. whole chicken
2 Tbsp. sesame oil
2 cloves garlic, minced
1/2 tsp. salt
1/4 tsp. black pepper
1/2 cup mango chunks, fresh or frozen
3/4 cup mango chutney
1/3 cup teriyaki sauce
1/2 cup water

Unwrap chicken, remove all giblets from cavities, and rinse thoroughly. Spray slow cooker or roasting pan (if using oven cooking method) with nonstick cooking spray.

In a small bowl, mix the sesame oil, garlic, salt and pepper, then rub mixture over the chicken. Drop the mango pieces in the cavity of the chicken. For mango sauce, combine the mango chutney and teriyaki sauce in a food processor or blender and process until smooth. Bake chicken as directed.

SLOW COOKER METHOD: Pour the 1/2 cup water into the slow cooker. Place chicken in the slow cooker and glaze with 1/4 cup mango sauce. Cook on LOW for 8 to 10 hours. Chicken should reach an internal temperature of 165°F. Serve with remaining mango sauce.

OVEN METHOD: Preheat oven to 350°F. Place chicken in prepared roasting pan. Glaze with 1/4 cup mango sauce. Roast for 1 hour, or until juice runs clear when pierced at thigh, basting with additional sauce during cooking. Chicken should reach an internal temperature of 165°F.

Serve with remaining mango sauce.

FREEZER PREPARATION: Prepare chicken as directed, but do not glaze with mango sauce and do not cook. Place chicken in one-gallon freezer bag; seal. Prepare mango sauce as directed and package in one-quart freezer bag or plastic container with tight-fitting lid. Label all and freeze.

ASIAN LETTUCE WRAPS

Serves 4

1 Tbsp. sesame oil
1 Tbsp. peanut oil

1 lb. ground chicken
3/4 cup minced green onions
2 tsp. cornstarch

1 cup water chestnuts, finely chopped
3 Tbsp. reduced sodium soy sauce
2 tsp. ground ginger
1 Tbsp. oyster sauce
1 Tbsp. hoisin sauce
2 tsp. sweet chili sauce
2 tsp. garlic chili sauce

Dipping Sauce:
1 1/2 tsp. lime juice
2 Tbsp. rice wine vinegar
1 dash Asian hot chili oil (optional)
1/4 cup sweet chile sauce
2 Tbsp. reduced sodium soy sauce
3 Tbsp. minced green onions
1 tsp. ground ginger
1 Tbsp. water

Lettuce leaves (Iceberg or Green Leaf Lettuce)
3/4 cup chow mein noodles

Heat oils in a large skillet over medium-high heat. Add chicken, breaking up pieces, and cook until no longer pink. Add green onions and cornstarch and continue cooking until chicken is cooked through.

Add next 7 ingredients and continue stirring over medium heat until well combined. Keep chicken mixture warm while making dipping sauce. For dipping sauce, mix lime juice and next 7 ingredients, stirring well.

To serve, spoon chicken mixture down the center of lettuce leaf; top with rice noodles and roll up. Serve with dipping sauce.

FREEZER PREPARATION: Place ground chicken in one-quart or one-gallon plastic freezer bag. Add minced green onion and cornstarch; seal. (Does not need to be mixed.) Mix water chestnuts and next six ingredients; place in one-quart freezer bag and seal. Mix all sauce ingredients and pour into deli container with tight-fitting lid. Portion rice noodles, if desired, into one-quart freezer bag and seal. Place all bags and containers into a two-gallon freezer bag; seal and label.

CHICKY KOWLOON

Serves 6-8

1 1/2 lbs. boneless, skinless chicken breasts, trimmed and cut into pieces

1 cup (about 6 ounces) pineapple chunks or tidbits in syrup, drained and syrup reserved
1/2 cup pineapple syrup (drained from canned pineapple)
1 5-ounce can water chestnuts
3/4 cup chicken broth
1 clove garlic, minced
1/4 tsp. ground ginger
1/4 tsp. black pepper
1/2 tsp. salt
1/2 cup sliced green onions

Sauce:
1/4 cup soy sauce
1 Tbsp. white vinegar
1/3 cup cornstarch

5 cups cooked Jasmine rice
2 cups (about 4 ounces) chow mein noodles

Spray slow cooker with nonstick cooking spray. Trim chicken pieces, if necessary, and place in slow cooker.

In a bowl, combine the pineapple, pineapple syrup, water chestnuts, chicken broth, garlic, ginger, pepper and salt. Mix well and pour over chicken in slow cooker. Cook on HIGH for 1 hour; reduce to LOW and cook for an additional 6 hours (or cook on low for 7 to 8 hours).

Add green onions to mixture in slow cooker. In a small bowl, whisk together Sauce ingredients, then stir into chicken mixture. Cook on HIGH for 10 minutes, or until slightly thickened.

Serve chicken over Jasmine rice, and top with chow mein noodles.

FREEZER PREPARATION: Prepare chicken as directed and place in one-gallon freezer bag. Prepare pineapple mixture as directed and pour over chicken in bag; seal tightly. Package sliced green onions in small bag; seal. Mix sauce ingredients and package in one-quart freezer bag or plastic container with tight-fitting lid. If desired, pre-cook rice; cook and package in one-gallon freezer bag. Portion chow mein noodles in small plastic bag; seal. Place all bags/containers in a two-gallon freezer bag; seal and label.

KUNG PAO CHICKEN

Serves 6

3 Tbsp. vegetable oil
8 dried red chiles

2 large boneless, skinless chicken breasts, trimmed & cut into small cubes or strips
3 Tbsp. oyster sauce
1 1/2 tsp. cornstarch

1/3 cup balsamic vinegar
1/3 cup chicken broth
1/4 cup dry sherry (not "cooking sherry")
3 Tbsp. hoisin sauce
1 1/2 Tbsp. soy sauce
1 Tbsp. sesame oil
1 Tbsp. chili garlic sauce
1 Tbsp. sugar

5 cloves garlic, minced
1 cup diced celery
3/4 cup red bell pepper, cut into 1" squares
1 1/4 cups diced bamboo shoots

1 Tbsp. cornstarch
1 Tbsp. water
1 Tbsp. chopped walnuts

5 cups cooked white rice

In a small bowl, soak the 8 dried red chiles in the 3 Tbsp. vegetable oil; set aside. In another bowl, mix the chicken pieces with 3 Tbsp. oyster sauce and 1 1/2 tsp. cornstarch; set aside. In a third bowl or large measuring cup, mix together the balsamic vinegar, chicken broth, sherry, hoisin sauce, soy sauce, sesame oil, chili garlic sauce and sugar; set aside.

Heat a large skillet over high heat. Add the red chiles in oil, then add the chicken and stri-fry for 3 minutes. Add garlic, celery, bell pepper and bamboo shoots and stir-fry another 2 minutes. Add the balsamic vinegar sauce and bring to a boil. Reduce heat to medium-low. Mix 1 Tbsp. cornstarch with 1 Tbsp. water; stir into pan and continue cooking until sauce thickens. Stir in walnuts. Serve over cooked rice.

FREEZER PREPARATION: Put red chiles in a resealable freezer bag and add oil; seal tightly. Put chicken pieces in a one-quart freezer bag and add the oyster sauce and cornstarch; seal. Mix the balsamic vinegar sauce as directed and pour into a one-quart freezer bag or plastic container with tight-fitting lid; seal. Put garlic, bell pepper, bamboo shoots and celery into a one-quart freezer bag; seal. Measure 1 Tbsp. cornstarch into a small plastic bag or deli cup; seal. Measure walnuts into a small plastic bag; seal. Cook rice and package in a one-gallon freezer bag; seal. Place all bags and containers in a two-gallon freezer bag.

SATAY PEANUT CHICKEN KABOBS

Serves 6

1/2 cup crunchy peanut butter
2 Tbsp. chopped cilantro
1/4 cup bottled chili sauce
1/2 tsp. salt
1/4 tsp. cayenne pepper
1/4 tsp. black pepper
2 Tbsp. lemon juice
2 Tbsp. firmly packed brown sugar
1/4 cup light soy sauce
1/4 cup minced green onions
3 cloves garlic, minced
1/2 cup water

4 large boneless, skinless chicken breasts (about 1 1/2 lbs.), rinsed and cut into 1' cubes
2 medium green bell peppers, cut into 1' square pieces
8 metal or bamboo skewers

Double sauce reserve 1/2 and heat serve with skewers.

In a large bowl, combine the peanut butter, cilantro, chili sauce, salt, cayenne, black pepper, lemon juice, brown sugar, soy sauce, green onions, garlic and water.

Thread chicken pieces and green pepper pieces on skewers (if using metal skewers, spray with nonstick cooking spray).

Lay skewers in a shallow baking dish. Pour the peanut butter marinade over and marinate skewers for at least 30 minutes, turning frequently to coat well.

Preheat grill to high heat (350°F to 400°F). Lay skewers on grill rack and cook for 5 to 6 minutes, turning once, or until chicken is just cooked through. To prevent burning, a sheet of foil may be placed on grill rack before adding the kabobs.

FREEZER PREPARATION: Prepare marinade and skewers as directed. Lay kabobs in shallow baking dish; pour marinade over. Cover tightly, label and freeze.

TURKEY EMPANADAS

Serves 6

2 cups cooked yellow rice
6 ounces cooked turkey, cut into 1/2" squares (can use deli turkey)
1 cup shredded Monterey Jack cheese
1/2 cup chopped green onions
1/2 cup sliced black olives
2 tsp. fajita seasoning
2 refrigerated pie crusts

Preheat oven to 400°F. Lay a sheet of foil or parchment on a cookie sheet.

In a large bowl, combine the cooked rice, turkey, Monterey Jack cheese, green onions, black olives and fajita seasoning.

Unroll pie crusts. Spread 1/2 of filling on each pie crust, putting filling on the bottom half of the round. Fold the top of the pie crust over, and seal the edges well, forming a half-moon shape. Cut 3 slits in each empanada to allow steam to escape.

Bake for 25 to 30 minutes or until golden brown. Serve with salsa.

FREEZER PREPARATION: Prepare empanada filling and package in a one-gallon freezer bag. Place bag of filling and wrapped crusts together in another one-gallon or a two-gallon freezer bag; label and freeze.

TURKEY TETRAZZINI

Serves 6

2 tsp. vegetable oil or butter
1/3 cup sliced or chopped fresh mushrooms
1 10.75-ounce can cream of mushroom soup
1 cup (8 ounces) prepared Alfredo sauce
3/4 cup chicken broth
1/4 cup dry sherry (do not use "cooking sherry")
1/2 cup shredded Parmesan cheese
1/4 tsp. black pepper
2 1/2 cups chopped cooked turkey
8 ounces vermicelli pasta, uncooked
1/3 cup Parmesan cheese

Preheat oven to 350°F. Spray a 9 x 13 baking pan with nonstick cooking spray.

Saute mushrooms in oil or butter for 2-3 minutes. In a large bowl, combine the soup, Alfredo sauce, chicken broth, sherry, Parmesan, pepper, sauteed mushrooms and cooked turkey.

Cook vermicelli according to package directions; drain (if pasta will sit before completing mixture, rinse the pasta with cool water). Stir pasta into sauce mixture and mix well. Spoon into prepared baking pan. Top with 1/3 cup Parmesan cheese.

Bake, uncovered, for 45 to 50 minutes or until hot and bubbly.

FREEZER PREPARATION: Prepare casserole as directed but do not bake. Cover dish tightly, label and freeze.

PLUM TURKEY MEDALLIONS

Serves 6

3/4 cup plum jam
1/4 cup dry sherry (do not use "cooking sherry")
2 Tbsp. olive oil
2 tsp. rosemary leaves, chopped, dried or fresh
1 1/2 tsp. garlic salt
1/4 tsp. black pepper
1/2 cup finely chopped onion

1 Tbsp. vegetable oil

1 1/2 lbs. turkey breast medallions (pre-packaged, or cut from boneless turkey breast)

In a small bowl, combine the plum jam, sherry, olive oil, rosemary, garlic salt, pepper and onions. Mix well. Pour half of plum mixture over turkey medallions in a separate dish or reclosable bag and marinate in refrigerator for 30 minutes or up to 24 hours.

Heat vegetable oil in a non-stick skillet over medium-high heat. Remove turkey from marinade and place in skillet. Cook 3 to 4 minutes per side (longer if turkey pieces are larger than 4 ounces), or until browned. Do not overcook turkey. Remove from pan.

Pour reserved plum sauce in skillet and heat. Pour heated sauce over cooked turkey to serve.

FREEZER PREPARATION: Mix plum sauce as directed. Pour half of sauce over turkey pieces in one-gallon freezer bag; seal and label. Pour remaining sauce into a one-quart freezer bag or plastic container with tight-fitting lid. Package both bags in one-gallon freezer bag; seal, label and freeze.

TURKEY with FLORENTINE STUFFING

Serves 6

1 1/2 to 2 lb. boneless turkey breast

2 1/4 cups (6 ounces) cornbread stuffing cubes
2 1/4 cups (6 ounces) white bread stuffing cubes
8 ounces frozen chopped spinach, thawed and well drained
1 cup chopped onion
1 cup chopped celery
1/4 cup walnut pieces, toasted
1/2 cup chopped apple
1/2 tsp. salt
1/4 tsp. pepper
1/4 tsp. ground nutmeg
1 15-ounce can chicken broth
1/4 cup butter, melted

2 Tbsp. melted butter
1 Tbsp. honey
1 tsp. dried thyme
2 cloves garlic, minced

Preheat oven to 350°F. Rinse turkey and set aside. Spray a 9 x 13 baking pan (or larger roasting pan) with nonstick cooking spray.

In a large bowl, mix stuffing cubes with spinach, onion, celery, walnut pieces, apple, salt, pepper and nutmeg. Stir in chicken broth and 1/4 cup melted butter. Spoon stuffing into prepared pan. Make an indention in the center of stuffing to accommodate the turkey breast. Lay the turkey breast on top of the stuffing; drizzle with 2 Tbsp. melted butter and 1 Tbsp. honey. Rub turkey with thyme and garlic.

Bake, uncovered, for 1 1/2 hours, or until turkey reaches internal temperature of 170°F.

FREEZER PREPARATION: Prepare stuffing and turkey as directed, but do not bake. Cover dish tightly, seal and label.

HERBED TURKEY BREAST

Serves 6

3/4 cup chicken broth
1/4 cup white wine
1 tsp. chicken base or bouillon granules
1 Tbsp. honey
1 tsp. thyme
1 tsp. rosemary
1 tsp. basil
1/2 tsp. salt
1/2 tsp. black pepper
4 garlic cloves, peeled and halved
1 tsp. Dijon mustard

1 2.5- to 3-lb. turkey breast

In a medium bowl, whisk together the chicken broth and next 10 ingredients. Place turkey breast in a one-gallon freezer bag; pour marinade over and marinate in refrigerator for 30 minutes, or up to 24 hours. Bake as directed.

SLOW COOKER METHOD: Spray slow cooker with nonstick cooking spray. Place turkey breast with marinade into slow cooker. Cook on LOW for 8 to 10 hours.

OVEN METHOD: Preheat oven to 350°F. Spray a roasting pan with cooking spray. Put turkey, with marinade, in pan and roast, uncovered, for 1 1/2 hours, or until turkey reaches an internal temperature of 165°F. Baste often with pan juices.

FREEZER PREPARATION: Prepare turkey as directed but do not bake. For extra protection, place bag with turkey inside another one-gallon freezer bag. Seal tightly and label.

PORK

GARLIC-PARMESAN PORK CHOPS

Serves 6

2 Tbsp. milk
1 1/4 Tbsp. Dijon mustard
2/3 cup Italian seasoned breadcrumbs
1/4 tsp. salt
1/4 tsp. black pepper

Six 4- to 6-ounce thick-cut boneless or bone-in pork chops

1 1/2 Tbsp. butter
1 clove garlic, minced
1 Tbsp. flour
2 Tbsp. chicken broth
1 1/2 Tbsp. white wine, or additional chicken broth
1/2 cup evaporated milk
1/2 cup grated Parmesan cheese

Preheat oven to 375°F. Spray a cookie sheet or shallow baking sheet with nonstick cooking spray, or line pan with foil and coat foil with cooking spray.

In a small bowl, whisk together the milk and Dijon mustard. Pour the breadcrumbs into a shallow pan and add the salt and pepper. Dip pork chops into milk mixture, then dredge in breadcrumbs, coating on both sides. Place pork chops on prepared baking sheet.

Bake pork chops for 35-40 minutes. While pork chops are baking, make sauce.

For sauce, melt butter with garlic in a small saucepan over medium-low heat. Whisk in flour until well mixed, then stir in chicken broth, white wine and evaporated milk. Continue stirring over medium-low heat until thickened, then stir in Parmesan cheese. Serve over cooked pork chops.

FREEZER PREPARATION: Prepare pork chops as directed and lay in 9 x 13 baking dish, layering with waxed paper if needed. Make sauce as directed and cool completely before freezing. Pour sauce into one-gallon freezer bag, or plastic container with tight-fitting lid. If possible, put sauce container in pan with pork chops. Cover all tightly, label and freeze.

SOUTHWESTERN GRILLED PORK CHOPS

Serves 6

6 center cut pork chops, bone-in or boneless, about 6 ounces each

1/4 cup lime juice
1 Tbsp. lemon juice
1 1/2 tsp. grated lime peel
1 tsp. ginger
1 Tbsp. sugar
3 Tbsp. chopped fresh cilantro
1/3 cup olive oil
1 garlic clove, minced

Compound Butter:
1/3 cup butter, softened
1 Tbsp. lime juice
1/2 tsp. grated lime peel
1 Tbsp. minced parsley
2 Tbsp. chopped fresh cilantro

Remove pork chops from package and put in a shallow dish with a cover, or in a one-gallon reclosable bag.

In a small bowl, whisk together the lime juice, lemon juice, lime peel, ginger, sugar, cilantro, olive oil and garlic. Pour over pork chops, cover dish (or seal bag) and marinate chops in refrigerator for at least 30 minutes or up to 24 hours.

For compound butter, mix all ingredients, cover and refrigerate until pork chops are cooked.

Preheat grill to medium-high. Remove pork chops from marinade, discarding marinade, and grill for 10 to 12 minutes per side, turning once. If pork chops are thinner than 3/4", decrease cooking time to 7 to 10 minutes per side. Pork should be an internal temperature of 160°F.

Serve cooked pork chops with a pat of compound butter.

FREEZER PREPARATION: Prepare marinade and pour over pork chops in a one-gallon freezer bag. Prepare compound butter as directed and package in a small plastic container with tight-fitting lid, or roll into a log and wrap tightly in plastic.

APPLE GLAZED PORK CHOPS

Serves 6

6 boneless pork chops, 1/2" to 1" thick
salt & pepper

1 21-ounce can apple pie filling
1 tsp. soy sauce
1 cup sliced onion
1/2 cup diced celery
1/2 cup ginger ale

1 tsp. cornstarch

Sprinkle pork chops with salt and pepper. Place pork chops in slow cooker that has been coated with nonstick cooking spray.

Combine apple pie filling, soy sauce, onion, celery and ginger ale; pour over the chops. Cook on HIGH for 2-3 hours, or LOW for 4-5 hours.

Mix cornstarch with 1 Tbsp. water; mix into apple mixture in slow cooker. Cook an additional 15 minutes to thicken sauce.

FREEZER PREPARATION: Sprinkle chops with salt and pepper; place chops into a one-quart freezer bag; seal. Combine apple pie filling, soy sauce, onions, celery and ginger ale; pour into a one-quart freezer bag; seal. Measure cornstarch in a 2-ounce deli cup or small plastic snack bag. Place all bags in a one-gallon freezer bag; seal, label and freeze.

SOUTHWESTERN PORK TENDERLOIN with ORANGE and BLACK BEAN SALSA

Serves 6

2 lbs. pork tenderloin
2 cloves garlic, minced
2 tsp. dried thyme
1 tsp. grated orange peel
1/2 cup orange juice
1/2 cup orange marmalade
3/4 cup fresh orange segments
1 cup black beans, drained and rinsed
1 cup diced red bell pepper
2 Tbsp. red wine vinegar
2 Tbsp. chopped fresh cilantro
2 Tbsp. minced jalapeno peppers

Remove pork from packaging and place in shallow dish with a cover, or in a one-gallon reclosable bag.

In a small bowl, whisk together garlic, thyme, orange peel, orange juice and marmalade. Pour over pork and marinate in refrigerator for at least 30 minutes, or up to 24 hours.

In a medium bowl, combine the fresh orange segments, black beans, red bell pepper, vinegar, cilantro and jalapenos. Set aside.

When ready to cook pork, preheat oven to 400°F. Spray a roasting pan with nonstick cooking spray, or line with foil and spray foil with cooking spray. Roast tenderloin, uncovered, for 40 to 45 minutes or until the pork reaches an internal temperature of 160°F.

To serve, slice pork into medallions and serve with Black Bean Salsa.

FREEZER PREPARATION: Prepare pork and marinade and package in a one-gallon freezer bag; seal tightly. Mix orange and black bean salsa as directed and package in a one-quart freezer bag; seal. Place both bags in another one-gallon freezer bag; label and freeze.

MARGARITA PORK TENDERLOIN

Serves 6

2 lbs. pork tenderloin
3 cloves garlic, minced
1/4 cup chopped green onions
1 Tbsp. minced jalapeno peppers (fresh or canned), seeds removed
3 Tbsp. finely chopped cilantro
2 Tbsp. lime juice
1 1/2 Tbsp. tequila
1 Tbsp. orange juice
1 tsp. salt
1 tsp. ground cumin
1/4 tsp. chili powder

Remove tenderloins from packaging and place in a glass dish or one-gallon reclosable bag.

In a small bowl, whisk together the garlic, green onions, jalapeno, cilantro, lime juice, tequila, orange juice, salt, cumin and chili powder. Pour over pork and marinate for at least 30 minutes, up to 24 hours (refrigerate if longer than 30 minutes).

Preheat grill to medium-high heat (350°F to 400°F). Grill tenderloin(s), covered, for 30 to 40 minutes, turning as needed, or until meat thermometer inserted in thickest portion registers 165°F. If meat begins to burn, place a sheet of foil beneath the meat. (Since performance of grills varies, cooking time may need to be adjusted.)

After removing meat from the grill, let rest for about 5 minutes before slicing into 1/2" to 1" slices.

FREEZER PREPARATION: Place pork with marinade in one-gallon freezer bag; seal tightly, label and freeze. (Do not cook.)

BOURBON PORK TENDERLOIN

Serves 6

1 3/4 to 2 lbs. pork tenderloins

3 Tbsp. reduced sodium soy sauce
3 Tbsp. Bourbon
2 Tbsp. brown sugar
4 cloves garlic, minced

Remove pork from packaging and place in a shallow dish with a cover, or in a reclosable plastic gallon bag.

In a small bowl, whisk together the soy sauce, Bourbon, brown sugar and garlic. Pour over tenderloins; marinate for at least 30 minutes or up to 24 hours.

Preheat oven to 375°F. Line a shallow roasting pan with foil and spray with nonstick cooking spray. Remove tenderloins from marinade (discard marinade) and roast for about 45 minutes, or until meat thermometer registers 165°F. Let meat rest for 5 minutes, then slice and serve.

To grill, preheat grill to medium-high heat. Grill tenderloin(s) for 30 to 40 minutes, turning once, until meat thermometer registers 165°. The sugar in the marinade can cause the grill to flare, so watch carefully to avoid burning. If necessary, place a piece of foil beneath the meat during cooking.

FREEZER PREPARATION: Mix marinade as directed and pour over meat in a one-gallon freezer bag; seal tightly, label and freeze.

ASIAN PORK TENDERLOIN

Serves 6 to 8

1 1/2 - 2 lbs. pork tenderloins

Marinade:
1/2 cup soy sauce
1/4 cup pineapple juice
1/4 cup chopped green onions
1/4 cup chopped cilantro
1 Tbsp. ground ginger
2 Tbsp. honey
2 Tbsp. rice wine vinegar
2 Tbsp. minced garlic
1 Tbsp. sesame oil
1 Tbsp. crushed red pepper flakes
1 tsp. Chinese Five-Spice seasoning
1 tsp. sugar

Remove tenderloins from original packaging and place in shallow dish or one-gallon freezer bag.

In a medium bowl, whisk together marinade ingredients, mixing well. Pour over tenderloins. Marinate for at least 30 minutes, and up to 24 hours. (Tenderloins can be frozen at this point.)

Preheat oven to 400° F. Spray roasting pan with nonstick cooking spray, or line with aluminum foil. Remove tenderloins from marinade, and discard marinade. Place tenderloins in prepared pan and bake for 30-40 minutes, or until internal temperature registers 165° F. Let meat rest for 5 minutes, then slice and serve.

GRILL METHOD: Preheat grill to medium-high. Place tenderloins on grill rack and cook for 30-40 minutes, turning as necessary, until internal temperature registers 165° F. Let meat rest for 5 minutes, then slice and serve.

FREEZER PREPARATION: Prepare marinade and tenderloin as directed in a one-gallon freezer bag. Do not cook. Seal, label and freeze.

APPLESAUCE PORK TENDERLOIN

Serves 6 to 8

2 lbs. pork tenderloins

1 to 2 tsp. vegetable oil
1 tsp. minced garlic
1/3 cup onion, diced
1/3 cup unsweetened applesauce
1/4 cup reduced sodium soy sauce
1/4 cup apple cider (can substitute apple juice)
1/2 tsp. ground ginger
1/2 tsp. black pepper

Preheat oven to 350° F.

Unwrap pork tenderloins and place in roasting pan coated with nonstick cooking spray or lined with foil.

Heat oil in a small skillet or saute pan. Saute garlic and onions for 2-3 minutes, or until tender. Stir in applesauce, soy sauce, cider, ginger and pepper. Spoon 1 cup glaze over tenderloins.

Bake for 50-60 minutes, or until internal temperature reaches 165° F, basting with remaining applesauce glaze. Let tenderloins stand 10 minutes before slicing.

FREEZER PREPARATION: Saute onions and garlic in oil as above; mix in applesauce, soy sauce, cider, ginger and pepper. Pour into one-quart plastic freezer bag; seal. Leave tenderloins in original packaging, or unwrap and transfer to one-gallon freezer bag. Place tenderloins and bag of sauce together into one-gallon freezer bag; seal, label and freeze.

PORK MEDALLIONS PICCATA

Serves 6

1 1/2 lbs. pork tenderloin

3/4 cup flour
2 tsp. lemon pepper

1/2 cup dry white wine
1/4 cup lemon juice
1/2 cup chicken broth
2 Tbsp. capers

Slice pork tenderloins into 1/4" thick medallions.

Mix flour and lemon pepper in a shallow dish. Toss medallions in flour mixture to coat.

Heat 2 Tbsp. butter or vegetable oil in a skillet over medium-high heat. Quickly saute medallions, turning once, until golden brown, about 7 to 8 minutes total.

In a small bowl, mix together the white wine, lemon juice, chicken broth and capers. Pour into skillet with cooked medallions. Reduce heat to medium-low and cook gently until sauce is thickened.

FREEZER PREPARATION: Slice pork tenderloin and package in a one-quart freezer bag; seal. Mix flour and lemon pepper and package in one-gallon freezer bag; seal. Mix white wine sauce as directed and package in one-quart freezer bag or plastic container with tight-fitting lid. Combine all packages in a one- or two- gallon freezer bag; seal, label and freeze.

CUBAN MOJO PORK ROAST

Serves 6

2 1/2 to 3 lb. boneless Boston butt pork roast

Marinade:
5 cloves garlic, minced
1 Tbsp. oregano
3/4 cup lime juice
1/2 cup orange juice
1 Tbsp. black pepper
2 tsp. salt
1/4 cup rice viengar
1/4 cup olive oil
2 Tbsp. chopped cilantro

Trim roast, if necessary, and place in a reclosable one-gallon bag. In a small bowl, thoroughly mix all marinade ingredients; pour over the roast and seal bag tightly. Marinate meat for at least 30 minutes, or up to 24 hours (preferable).

Slow Cooker Method: Spray slow cooker with nonstick cooking spray. Place roast in slow cooker and pour liquid over and around roast. Cook on LOW for 8 to 10 hours, or until meat is tender.

Oven Method: Preheat oven to 350°F. Place roast and liquid in a large roasting pan and cover with foil. Bake for 2 hours, uncover and bake an additional 30 minutes.

FREEZER PREPARATION: Prepare roast and marinade as directed, but do not bake. Seal bag tightly, label and freeze.

HEAVENLY HAM CASSEROLE

Serves 6-8

8 ounces egg noodles
1 10.75-ounce can cream of mushroom soup
6 ounces cream cheese, softened
1 tsp. onion powder
1 Tbsp. chopped chives
1/2 cup milk
1/1/4 cups chopped baked ham
1 cup broccoli florets, fresh or frozen
3/4 cup shredded carrot
1 1/2 cups shredded Mozzarella cheese, divided
3/4 cup shredded Cheddar cheese, divided
1/2 cup seasoned croutons, crushed

Preheat oven to 375°F. Spray a 9 x 13 baking pan with nonstick cooking spray.

Cook noodles according to package directions; drain, rinse and set aside.

In a large bowl, combine soup, cream cheese, onion powder, chives and milk. Mix thoroughly, then stir in cooked noodles, ham, broccoli, carrots, 1 cup Mozzarella cheese and 1/2 cup Cheddar cheese. Pour mixture into prepared pan. Top with crushed croutons and remaining cheese.

Bake, uncovered, for 30 to 40 minutes or until heated through.

FREEZER PREPARATION: Prepare as directed but do not bake. Cover tightly, label and freeze.

GUMBO POT PIE

Serves 6-8

1 lb. boneless, skinless chicken breast, trimmed and cut into 1/2" cubes
8 ounces kielbasa sausage, cut into 1/4" slices
1 cup diced onion
1 cup diced red bell pepper
1/2 cup diced celery

1/4 cup flour
2 Tbsp. roux concentrate
1/2 tsp. thyme
1 tsp. black pepper
1 Tbsp. paprika
1 tsp. salt

1/2 tsp. garlic powder
1/4 tsp. cayenne pepper
2 cups chicken broth
1 cup diced tomatoes, drained if using canned
1/2 cup sliced okra

1 frozen puff pastry sheet, thawed
1 egg, beaten
1 Tbsp. dried parsley
1 Tbsp. grated Parmesan cheese

Preheat oven to 375°F. Spray a 9 x 13 baking pan with nonstick cooking spray.

In a large skillet, over medium-high heat, saute the diced chicken and Kielbasa sausage for 4 to 5 minutes. Remove from the skillet and drain, leaving any sausage drippings in the skillet. Using the same pan, saute the onion, bell pepper and celery for 3 to 4 minutes. Stir in the flour, roux concentrate, thyme, black pepper, paprika, salt, garlic powder, cayenne pepper, chicken broth, diced tomatoes and okra. Stir in the chicken and sausage. Turn off heat.

Pour mixture from skillet into prepared baking pan. Top with sheet of puff pastry, trimming to fit if necessary. Cut 6 slits in the top of pastry. Brush with beaten egg and sprinkle with parsley and grated Parmesan.

Bake, uncovered, for 45 minutes or until pastry is golden brown. Let pie rest 5 to 10 minutes before serving.

FREEZER PREPARATION: Prepare as directed but do not bake. Cover dish tightly, seal and label.

ORANGE GLAZED COUNTRY STYLE RIBS

Serves 6

1 3/4 to 2 lbs. boneless country style pork loin ribs
2/3 cup onion slices
1 clove garlic, minced

1/2 cup orange marmalade
3 Tbsp. soy sauce
1/2 cup diced green bell pepper
2 Tbsp. cornstarch
1 tsp. ground ginger

Spray a slow cooker with nonstick cooking spray. Place ribs, onion slices and garlic in slow cooker. Cover, cook on LOW for 8 to 9 hours.

While ribs are cooking, mix together the marmalade, soy sauce, bell pepper, cornstarch and ginger. Mix in 3/4 cup juices from slow cooker. Heat for 2 to 2 1/2 minutes in a microwave, or simmer on medium-low in a small saucepan.

Serve cooked ribs with sauce.

FREEZER PREPARATION: Package ribs with onions and garlic in a one-gallon freezer bag; seal. Mix sauce as directed and package in a plastic container with tight-fitting lid, or in a one-quart freezer bag. Combine both bags in another one-gallon freezer bag; seal, label and freeze.

SAUCY BARBECUE RIBS

Serves 6

2 lbs. country-style pork ribs, trimmed

1/2 cup chopped onion
1/2 cup light brown sugar, firmly packed
1/2 cup apple butter
1/2 cup ketchup
1/4 cup lemon juice
1/4 cup orange juice
1 1/2 tsp. bottled steak sauce
1/2 tsp. black pepper
1 clove garlic, minced
1/4 tsp. Worcestershire sauce

In a medium bowl, mix together the chopped onion, brown sugar, apple butter, ketchup, lemon juice, orange juice, steak sauce, black pepper, garlic and Worcestershire sauce.

Spray the inside of a slow cooker with nonstick cooking spray. Place ribs in slow cooker. Pour sauce over the ribs, cover and cook on HIGH for 6 to 7 hours. If cooking a smaller amount, or if recipe does not fill up the slow cooker, lower heat and monitor cooking so that ribs do not dry out.

FREEZER PREPARATION: Package ribs in a one-gallon freezer bag. Mix up sauce as directed and package in a one-gallon freezer bag; seal tightly. Combine both bags in another one- or two-gallon freezer bag; label and freeze.

JAPANESE PORK STIR-FRY

Serves 6

1 lb. pork tenderloin or 2 boneless center cut pork chops, cut into 1/2" wide strips
1 Tbsp. teriyaki sauce

1 cup chicken broth
1/3 cup low sodium soy sauce
2 Tbsp. sugar
1 clove garlic, minced
3/4 tsp. ground ginger

1 Tbsp. vegetable oil
4 cups frozen stir-fry vegetables
1 cup fresh snow peas
3 Tbsp. chopped red bell pepper
2 Tbsp. cornstarch
2 Tbsp. water

5 cups cooked Jasmine rice, brown rice, or whole wheat angel hair pasta

Place pork strips in a medium bowl and toss with teriyaki sauce. Set aside. In a small bowl, whisk together the broth, soy sauce, sugar, garlic and ginger; set aside.

Heat the vegetable oil in a large nonstick skillet over medium-high to high heat. Add pork strips and stir-fry 3 to 4 minutes. Add vegetables and stir-fry 2 to 3 more minutes. Add sauce, reduce heat to medium-low and stir well to combine. In a small bowl, mix the cornstarch and water; add to the pan and cook a few more minutes until thickened.

Serve over cooked rice or pasta.

FREEZER PREPARATION: Package pork strips with teriyaki in one-quart freezer bag. Mix sauce as directed and package in a plastic container with tight-fitting lid. Combine all vegetables in a one-gallon freezer bag; seal. Measure cornstarch (no water) in a small bag or deli cup; seal. Package pre-cooked rice or pasta in a one-gallon freezer bag; seal. Combine all bags in a one- or two-gallon freezer bag; seal, label and freeze.

MU SHU WRAPS

Serves 6

1 1/2 lbs. lean ground pork

4 1/2 tsp. soy sauce
3 Tbsp. lime juice
1 1/2 Tbsp. honey
3/4 tsp. crushed red pepper flakes

1 1/2 tsp. sesame oil
3 cups shredded cabbage and carrots (slaw mixture)
1 thinly sliced onion
1 tsp. ground ginger
2 cloves garlic, minced

6 10" flour tortillas

Cook ground pork in a skillet until no longer pink, and cooked through (about 8 minutes). Drain.

In a small bowl or measuring cup, whisk together the soy sauce, lime juice, honey and red pepper flakes.

In the same skillet used for cooking pork, heat the sesame oil over medium-high heat. Add the cabbage and carrots, onion, ginger and garlic, and saute 3-4 minutes, or until vegetables begin to wilt. Pour in sauce and stir-fry for 1 minute, then add the pork and cook an additional 1 to 2 minutes or until heated through.

Heat tortillas in oven or microwave. To serve, fill each tortilla with pork and vegetable mixture, fold over sides about 1", then roll the tortilla around the filling.

FREEZER PREPARATION: After cooking pork, package in one-quart freezer bag. Mix sauce as directed and package in plastic container with tight-fitting lid; seal. Toss together cabbage and carrots, onion, ginger and garlic and package in one-gallon freezer bag; seal. Wrap tortillas in plastic wrap. Package all bags in a two-gallon freezer bag; seal and label.

GINGERED PORK with PEANUT SAUCE

Serves 6

1 lb. pork tenderloin or boneless pork chops
2 Tbsp. olive oil
3/4 tsp. red pepper flakes
2 tsp. ground ginger

2 pkgs. pork flavored oriental noodles (Ramen or other brand)

4 Tbsp. peanut butter
3 Tbsp. soy sauce
2 Tbsp. coconut milk
1/2 cup broth from cooked noodles

1 cup (about 4 ounces) frozen chopped spinach, thawed and drained well
1/2 cup chopped green onions

Trim pork of any extra fat; slice pork into 1/4" slices, then cut each slice in half. Place pork strips in a bowl and toss with olive oil, red pepper flakes and ginger.

Prepare oriental noodles according to package directions. Reserve 1/2 cup broth, then drain noodles.

In a small bowl, mix the peanut butter, soy sauce, coconut milk and reserved 1/2 cup broth.

Spray a large skillet with nonstick cooking spray and place over high heat. Add seasoned pork and stir fry for about 4 minutes, or until pork is tender. Reduce heat to medium, then stir in the spinach, green onions and peanut sauce. Stir in the noodles and mix until all ingredients are combined and heated through.

FREEZER PREPARATION: Prepare pork as directed and combine with oil and seasonings. Package in a one-quart freezer bag; seal tightly. Leave noodles in original packaging. Mix the peanut sauce as directed and package in a one-quart freezer bag or plastic container with tight-fitting lid. Seal. Portion spinach and green onion together in a separate freezer bag; seal. Place all bags, including Ramen noodles, in a one-gallon freezer bag; seal tightly and label.

BEEF

KANE'S PERFECT MEATLOAF

Serves 6

1/2 cup diced onions
2 tsp. vegetable oil
2 lbs. ground beef
2 garlic cloves, minced
1 egg
1 tsp. vegetable oil
2 tsp. Dijon mustard
2 tsp. Worcestershire sauce
1/4 tsp. Tabasco
1/2 cup milk
1/2 tsp. dried thyme
1/3 cup minced parsley (dried or fresh)
1 tsp. salt
1/2 tsp. black pepper
2/3 cup crushed saltine crackers

Glaze:
1/2 cup ketchup
4 Tbsp. brown sugar
4 tsp. vinegar
4 tsp. Worcestershire sauce

Preheat oven to 350°F. Spray a 9 x 13 baking pan with nonstick cooking spray.

In a small skillet, saute the onions in vegetable oil until soft. (Or saute in the microwave for 1-2 minutes in a microwave-safe dish.)

In a large bowl, mix the ground beef with the sauteed onions, garlic, egg, oil, Dijon mustard, Worcestershire, Tabasco, milk, thyme, parsley, salt, pepper and crushed saltines. Mix thoroughly and divide into 4 pieces. Shape each piece into a small loaf and place in prepared pan. Mix all glaze ingredients in a small bowl, and spoon over each loaf.

Bake, uncovered, for 1 hour.

FREEZER PREPARATION: Prepare as directed but do not bake. Cover dish tightly, label and freeze.

SHEPHERD'S PIE

Serves 6

1 1/2 lbs. ground beef
1/2 tsp. salt
1/4 tsp. black pepper
3/4 cup prepared brown gravy (can be homemade, canned or prepared from dry mix)
1 3/4 cups (about 8 ounces) frozen peas and carrots
3 1/2 cups prepared mashed potatoes
2 Tbsp. milk
1 Tbsp. butter, melted
1 cup shredded Cheddar cheese

Preheat oven to 375°F. Spray a 9 x 13 baking pan with nonstick cooking spray.

Cook ground beef in skillet until browned and loses its pink color. Season with salt and pepper. Drain, then spread ground beef over the bottom of prepared pan. Stir in the prepared brown gravy. Top with the frozen peas and carrots.

In a large bowl, mix the mashed potatoes with the milk, butter and Cheddar cheese. Spoon mashed potato mixture over the peas and carrots, then carefully spread evenly to the edges of the dish.

Bake, uncovered, for 25 to 30 minutes or until lightly browned.

FREEZER PREPARATION: Prepare casserole as directed but do not bake. Cover dish tightly; seal, label and freeze.

BEEF AND POTATO CASSEROLE

Serves 6-8

1 lb. ground beef

1 14-oz. can cream of mushroom soup
1/2 cup milk

4 cups potato slices, fresh or frozen
1/2 tsp. black pepper
1 cup shredded Cheddar cheese
2 cups green beans, canned, frozen or fresh

1 cup French fried onions

Preheat oven to 350°F. Spray a 9 x 13 baking pan with nonstick cooking spray.

Brown ground beef in medium skillet until no longer pink; drain and set aside (salt if desired).

In a medium bowl, combine cream of mushroom soup and milk and mix thoroughly.

In prepared pan, layer the sliced potatoes, black pepper, Cheddar cheese, green beans and cooked ground beef. Pour soup and milk mixture over the entire casserole, then top with the French fried onions.

Bake uncovered for 50 minutes or until potatoes are tender.

FREEZER PREPARATION: If freezing this dish, use pre-packed frozen potato slices, or par-boil fresh potatoes for 4-5 minutes before preparing dish. (Freezing will cause fresh potatoes to turn gray.) Prepare dish as directed, cover tightly and label.

COLORADO STYLE BEEF ENCHILADAS

Serves 8

1 1/4 lb. ground beef
3/4 cup diced onion
3 Tbsp. taco seasoning
1/4 tsp. black pepper
1/4 cup diced green chiles
3/4 cup salsa verde
1/4 cup water

1 1/4 cups mild red enchilada sauce
1 1/4 cups mild green enchilada sauce
1/3 cup sour cream
3 Tbsp. milk

12 corn tortillas

1 1/4 cups shredded Cheddar cheese
1 1/4 cups shredded Monterey Jack cheese

Preheat oven to 350°F. Spray a 9 x 13 baking pan with nonstick cooking spray.

Brown ground beef with onions until meat is no longer pink. Drain. Return meat to the pan and add the taco seasoning, pepper, green chiles, salsa verde and water. Cover and simmer over low heat for 15 minutes.

In a medium bowl, mix together the enchilada sauces, sour cream and milk. Spread 3/4 cup of the sauce over the bottom of prepared pan. To assemble, lay four corn tortillas in the bottom of the dish, then top with 1 cup meat mixture, 1/3 cup Cheddar cheese and 1/3 cup Monterey Jack cheese. Repeat tortillas, meat and cheese for two additional layers.

Pour remaining enchilada sauce mix over the casserole, then top with remaining cheese.

Bake, uncovered, for 30 to 40 minutes. Let rest 5 minutes before serving.

FREEZER PREPARATION: Prepare casserole as directed but do not bake. Cover tightly, seal and freeze.

FIESTA CASSEROLE

Serves 6

1 1/2 lbs. ground beef
3/4 cup chopped onion
1 tsp. garlic salt
2 tsp. chili powder
1 tsp. black pepper
1 15-ounce can Ranch Style Beans, or chili beans, not drained

12 corn tortillas

1 cup shredded Cheddar cheese
1 10.75-ounce can cream of chicken soup
1 10-ounce can diced tomatoes with green chiles

Preheat oven to 350°F. Spray a 9 x 13 baking pan with nonstick cooking spray.

In a skillet, brown the ground beef with the chopped onion until beef loses its pink color. Drain off grease. Return beef to skillet and stir in garlic salt, chili powder, black pepper and Ranch Style Beans. Mix well.

Spread one spoonful of beef mixture on the bottom of prepared pan. Lay 6 corn tortillas in the dish, cutting to fit, if necessary. Spoon the ground beef mixture over the tortillas. Top with the shredded cheese, then the remaining 6 corn tortillas.

In a bowl, mix together the cream of chicken soup and diced tomatoes. Spread over the top of the corn tortillas.

Bake, uncovered, for 40-45 minutes or until heated through.

FREEZER PREPARATION: Prepare casserole as directed but do not bake. Cover dish well, label and freeze.

LA BAMBA CASSEROLE

Serves 6

22 green chile strips, or 12 ounces chopped green chiles
1 lb. ground beef
1/2 cup chopped onions
2 tsp. chili powder
1/2 tsp. cumin
1/2 tsp. salt
1 clove garlic, minced
3/4 cup diced tomatoes with green chiles
1/2 cup (4 ounces) tomato sauce
2 cups corn
1 16-ounce can refried beans
1 1/4 cups shredded Cheddar cheese

Preheat oven to 350°F. Spray a 9 x 13 baking pan with nonstick cooking spray. Arrange green chiles in a single layer over the bottom of the pan.

In a large skillet, cook the ground beef with the onions; drain. Stir in the chili powder, cumin, salt, garlic, tomatoes with green chiles and tomato sauce. Spoon the meat mixture over the green chiles. Top with the corn. Drop spoonfuls of the refried beans over the top of the corn, then spread carefully to the edges of the pan. Top with the Cheddar cheese.

Bake, uncovered, for 30 to 40 minutes. Good served with warm tortillas and sour cream.

FREEZER PREPARATION: Prepare as directed but do not bake. Cover dish tightly, label and freeze.

FIRECRACKER CASSEROLE

Serves 8

2 lbs. ground beef
1/2 cup diced onion
1 Tbsp. chili powder
1 to 3 tsp. cumin (to taste)
1 tsp. salt
1 15-ounce can Ranch Style beans
6 corn tortillas, cut into sixths
1 cup shredded Cheddar cheese
1 cup shredded Monterey Jack cheese
1 10-ounce can diced tomatoes with chiles
1 10.75-ounce can cream of mushroom soup

Preheat oven to 350°F. Spray a 9 x 13 baking pan with nonstick cooking spray.

Brown ground beef with diced onions; drain off grease, then season with chili powder, cumin and salt. Spoon beef into prepared baking pan, then layer the following over: Ranch Style beans, corn tortilla pieces, Cheddar cheese, Monterey Jack cheese, diced tomatoes with green chiles and cream of mushroom soup.

Bake, uncovered, for 40 to 45 minutes, or until bubbly and heated through.

FREEZER PREPARATION: Prepare casserole as directed, but do not bake. Cover tightly, seal and label.

BEEF and BOWTIE SKILLET

Serves 4 to 6

1 lb. ground beef
1 15-ounce can beef broth
1 14-ounce can diced tomatoes with juice
1 tsp. salt
2 tsp. Italian seasoning
2 cups bowtie pasta (farfalle), uncooked
2 cups fresh zucchini pieces (slice thick, then cut in halves or quarters

3/4 cup grated Parmesan cheese

In a large skillet over medium heat, brown the ground beef until no longer pink; drain. Return the empty skillet to the heat and add the beef broth, tomatoes, salt and Italian seasoning. Stir in the pasta. Bring to a boil; reduce heat to medium and cook, uncovered, for 15 minutes, stirring frequently.

Add zucchini and continue cooking for an additional 5 minutes or until pasta is tender. Stir in cooked beef and 1/2 cup of Parmesan cheese and heat through.

Top each serving with additional Parmesan cheese.

FREEZER PREPARATION: Cook ground beef; drain, cool and package in one-quart freezer bag. Combine beef broth, tomatoes and seasonings in a one-gallon freezer bag; seal tightly. Portion dry pasta, zucchini pieces and grated Parmesan separately in freezer bags; seal. Combine all bags in a one- or two-gallon freezer bag; seal, label and freeze.

MICROWAVE STUFFED PEPPERS

Serves 6

6 green bell peppers

1 lb. ground beef
1/2 cup water
1/4 cup tomato sauce
1/4 cup taco seasoning mix

2 cups cooked mashed potatoes
6 Tbsp. shredded Cheddar cheese
1 tsp. black pepper

Prepare bell peppers by cutting in half lengthwise, pull off stem, then remove all seeds and white membranes from inside. Rinse and dry.

Brown ground beef in a skillet over medium-high heat until no longer pink; drain. Return beef to pan and add water, tomato sauce and taco seasoning mix. Cook until liquid has evaporated; cool.

To assemble, lay pepper halves, cut side up, in a microwave-safe baking dish. Fill each pepper with the ground beef mixture, then top with 1/3 cup mashed potatoes and 1 Tbsp. cheddar cheese. Sprinkle black pepper over each one.

To cook, add 2 Tbsp. water to the bottom of the baking dish, then cover with plastic wrap, venting at one corner. Microwave on HIGH for 8 minutes. (Microwave ovens vary, so cooking time and temperature may need adjustment.) Peppers may be baked in a conventional oven at 350°F for 20 to 30 minutes.

FREEZER PREPARATION: Prepare peppers as directed but do not bake. Lay in a freezer container and cover tightly; label and freeze.

BEEF STROGANOFF

Serves 6

1 1/4 lb. beef sirloin cubes, or other lean stew meat, cut into 1" cubes
2 cups beef broth, or 2 beef bouillon cubes dissolved in 2 cups water

2 tsp. vegetable oil or butter
1/2 cup diced onions

2 10.75-ounce cans cream of mushroom soup
1 cup milk
1 cup evaporated milk
1/2 cup sour cream
1/2 cup plain (unsweetened) yogurt

1 tsp. prepared mustard
1/4 tsp. black pepper
2 tsp. beef base, or 2 bouillon cubes
1 Tbsp. tomato paste

10 ounces medium egg noodles

SLOW COOKER METHOD: Place beef cubes and 2 cups beef broth in slow cooker. Cook 8-10 hours on Low heat, or until beef is tender. Check beef from time to time to be sure pieces on top are not drying out. (This step can be done 1 day ahead.) Pour liquid off of beef pieces, leaving beef in slow cooker.

Saute onions in oil or butter in a small skillet, or microwave on high 2-3 minutes. In a large bowl, combine onions, cream of mushroom soup, milk, evaporated milk, sour cream, yogurt, mustard, pepper, beef base and tomato paste. Pour mixture over beef in slow cooker and cook 2-3 hours on LOW.

About 20 minutes before serving, cook noodles according to package directions. Serve stroganoff over noodles.

OVEN METHOD: Place beef cubes and 2 cups beef broth in ovenproof Dutch oven. Bake, covered, at 350°F for 1 1/2 to 2 hours or until beef is tender. When done, pour liquid off and leave beef in pan. Prepare onions and sauce ingredients as directed above and pour over beef. Return to oven and cook an additional 45 minutes to 1 hour, or until heated through. Serve over cooked noodles as directed above.

FREEZER PREPARATION: Pre-cook beef cubes in slow cooker or oven; drain off liquid and package beef in one-quart freezer bag. Seal tightly. Saute onions, then mix with all sauce ingredients. Package sauce in one-gallon freezer bag and seal tightly (double-bag if desired). Cook noodles according to package directions; drain. Toss noodles with small amount of vegetable or olive oil to prevent sticking. Package in one-gallon freezer bag. Combine all three bags in a 2-gallon freezer bag; seal and label.

BEEF BURGUNDY

Serves 6

2 Tbsp. vegetable oil
1 1/2 lbs. beef sirloin cubes, cut into 1" pieces

1/4 cup water
1 cup Burgundy wine
1/2 tsp. beef base, or 1 beef bouillon cube
1/2 tsp. salt
1/4 tsp. black pepper
1 bay leaf
1/2 tsp. thyme
2 cloves garlic, minced
2 cups sliced mushrooms
1 cup onion slices

2 Tbsp. cornstarch
2 Tbsp. water

8 ounces medium egg noodles, cooked

SLOW COOKER METHOD: In a large skillet, brown beef cubes in oil. Spray slow cooker with nonstick cooking spray, then add beef cubes. Add water, Burgundy wine, beef base, salt, pepper, bay leaf, thyme, garlic, mushrooms and onions. Cook on LOW for 8 to 10 hours. Remove bay leaf. Mix 2 Tbsp. cornstarch with 2 Tbsp. water and mix into stew. Cook on HIGH an additional 15 minutes. Serve over cooked noodles.

OVEN METHOD: Brown beef cubes in oil in Dutch oven coated with nonstick cooking spray. Add water, Burgundy wine, beef base, salt, pepper, bay leaf, thyme, garlic, mushrooms and onions. Bake, covered, at 325°F for 2-3 hours, or until tender. Remove bay leaf. Mix 2 Tbsp. cornstarch with 2 Tbsp. water and mix into stew during last 30 minutes of cooking time. Serve over cooked noodles.

FREEZER PREPARATION: Package beef cubes in one-quart freezer bag; seal. In a bowl, mix water, Burgundy wine, beef base, salt, pepper, bay leaf, thyme, garlic, mushrooms and onions. Pour into one-gallon freezer bag; seal tightly. If desired, package 2 Tbsp. cornstarch in small deli cup or small plastic bag. Cook noodles according to package directions; drain, rinse and cool. Toss noodles with small amount of vegetable or olive oil to prevent sticking. Package in one-gallon freezer bag. Place all bags/containers in one-gallon or two-gallon freezer bag; seal and label.

BALSAMIC FLANK STEAK

Serves 6

1/3 cup balsamic vinegar
2 Tbsp. brown sugar
1/2 tsp. salt

One 2-lb. flank steak, trimmed of any excess fat

1/2 cup dried parsley (or 1 cup fresh)
1 cup cilantro
1/3 cup olive oil
1/4 cup lime juice
1/4 tsp. salt
1 pinch crushed red pepper flakes

> **Handy Tip:**
>
> Flank steak becomes tough if overcooked. For steaks 1" to 1 1/4" thick, cook for no longer than 10 minutes per side. If thinner, reduce cooking time by 2-3 minutes per each 1/4". Check steaks during cooking; meat should be dark pink in the center.

Preheat grill to medium-high heat. Place flank steak in one-gallon reclosable plastic bag or shallow dish.

In a small bowl or large mixing cup, combine balsamic vinegar, brown sugar and salt. Mix well and pour over flank steak. Marinate for 30 minutes (or up to overnight).

In a separate bowl, mix parsley, cilantro, olive oil, lime juice, salt and red pepper flakes.

Grill flank steak, covered, for 6-7 minutes on each side, turning once, or to desired doneness. (Watch carefully to avoid burning.) Be careful not to overcook flank steak, or meat will become tough.

Let steak rest for 5 minutes, then slice steak diagonally across the grain into thin slices. Serve with Parsley-Cilantro Sauce.

FREEZER PREPARATION: Prepare marinade and directed, and pour over flank steak in one-gallon freezer bag; seal tightly. Prepare Parsley-Cilantro Sauce as directed and pour into one-quart freezer bag or plastic container with lid; seal tightly and label. Place flank steak and sauce together into a one-gallon freezer bag; seal and label.

HERB CRUSTED FLANK STEAK

Serves 6

1 1.5- to 2-lb. flank steak
1/4 cup lemon juice
1/4 cup Dijon mustard
1 tsp. coarse ground black pepper
1/3 cup fine dry breadcrumbs
1/3 cup shredded Parmesan cheese
1 1/2 Tbsp. butter, melted
3 Tbsp. dried parsley
3 Tbsp. dried basil

Handy Tip:

Flank steak becomes tough if overcooked. For steaks 1" to 1 1/4" thick, cook for no longer than 10 minutes per side. If thinner, reduce cooking time by 2-3 minutes per each 1/4". Check steaks during cooking; meat should be dark pink in the center.

Lay flank steak on a piece of waxed paper. Score the surface of the meat on both sides. To do this, run a sharp knife across the surface of the steak, making very shallow cuts from side to side, on the diagonal and spaced about 1" apart. Rotate the steak and make another set of cuts, forming a wide "X" pattern. (These cuts should not be deep -- they should only break the surface of the meat.)

In a small bowl, mix the lemon juice, Dijon mustard and black pepper. Remove 2 Tbsp. of this mixture and place in another small bowl, then add the breadcrumbs, Parmesan, butter, parsley and basil; mix well. Pour the lemon mixture from the first bowl over the flank steak. Spoon the breadcrumb mixture over the top of the steak, pressing to adhere. Bake or grill as directed.

OVEN METHOD: Preheat broiler to 450°F. Line a broiler pan with foil and spray with nonstick cooking spray. Place steak on foil and broil for 20 minutes (decrease time if steak is less than 1.5 lbs.). Meat should reach an internal temperature of 160°F to 170°F. Top will be crusty and brown. If topping browns too quickly, lower the oven rack.

GRILL METHOD: Preheat grill to high heat. Lay a piece of foil on grill rack, and place flank steak on foil. Grill, covered, for 20 minutes (or to proper internal temperature noted above). DO NOT TURN!

FREEZER PREPARATION: Prepare as directed. Place steak in freezer pan, cover tightly, label and freeze.

SOUTH of the BORDER STEAK

Serves 6

1/3 cup lemon juice
1/3 cup olive oil
6 Tbsp. minced jalapeno peppers, fresh or canned
1 to 2 Tbsp. chopped fresh cilantro
1 tsp. salt
1 tsp. black pepper

2 1/4 to 2 1/2 lb. flank steak, trimmed (for additional servings, allow 6 ounces per serving)

In a small bowl or large measuring cup, whisk together the lemon juice, olive oil, jalapenos, cilantro, salt and pepper.

Remove flank steak from packaging and place in shallow dish with a cover, or in a one-gallon reclosable bag. Pour marinade over. Seal dish or bag and marinate in refrigerator for at least 30 minutes or up to 24 hours (the longer the marinating time, the better the flavor).

Preheat grill to medium-high heat. Remove steak from marinade, discarding marinade, and grill flank steak for 7 to 10 minutes per side, turning once. If cooking a steak smaller than 2 1/2 pounds, decrease cooking time to 5 to 7 minutes per side. Do not overcook, or steak will become tough.

After removing steak from grill, let rest for about 5 minutes, then slice thinly across the grain to serve.

FREEZER PREPARATION: Prepare marinade, then package raw steak with marinade in a one-gallon freezer bag. Seal; label and freeze.

SAUCY BEEF BRISKET

Serves 6 to 7

3 lb. boneless beef brisket, trimmed

1 cup diced onion
2 Tbsp. vegetable oil
1 3/4 cups ketchup
3/4 cup packed brown sugar
1/4 cup Worcestershire sauce
2 1/2 Tbsp. lemon juice
1 Tbsp. chili powder
3/4 tsp. bottled hot pepper sauce
1/2 tsp. horseradish
1/2 tsp. salt
1/4 tsp. garlic powder

1 Tbsp. Liquid Smoke
1/4 cup steak seasoning (such as Montreal Steak seasoning)

Preheat oven to 225°F. Spray a 9 x 13 baking pan with nonstick cooking spray. Place brisket in prepared pan, fat side up.

In a large bowl, whisk together the onion, oil, ketchup, brown sugar, Worcestershire, lemon juice, chili powder, hot pepper sauce, horseradish, salt and garlic powder.

Brush brisket with Liquid Smoke, then sprinkle with steak seasoning. Pour at least 1 cup sauce over brisket, enough to cover meat completely.

Bake, covered, for 10 to 12 hours (works well to put in the oven overnight). Remove brisket from pan and place on cutting board. Let rest 5 to 10 minutes before slicing. Heat extra sauce on top of stove or in microwave.

FREEZER PREPARATION: Prepare meat as directed but do not bake. Cover dish tightly, seal and freeze. Package extra sauce in plastic container with tight-fitting lid.

BEEF KABOBS IN SHERRY MARINADE

Serves 6

1 1/4 cup dry sherry (not "Cooking Sherry" found in grocery vinegar section)
3/4 cup olive oil
1/2 cup reduced sodium soy sauce
2 tsp. minced garlic
1/2 tsp. ground black pepper

1 1/2 lbs. beef sirloin, cut into 1 1/2" cubes

1 cup mushrooms
1 cup each, red & green bell pepper, cut into 1 1/2" pieces
1 cup onion pieces (quartered)

8 metal or bamboo skewers, 10" long

In a small bowl, mix the dry sherry, olive oil, soy sauce, garlic and black pepper. Add the beef and marinate for about 30 minutes. If using wooden skewers, soak skewers in water while beef is marinating.

Thread sirloin cubes and vegetables onto skewers, alternating beef and vegetables.

Preheat grill to 350° to 400°F. Grill kabobs, covered, for 5 to 7 minutes on each side, or to desired doneness.

FREEZER PREPARATION: Prepare marinade as directed. Thread beef onto skewers, alternating beef and vegetables. Lay kabobs in 9 x 13 pan; pour marinade over. Seal and label.

BALSAMICO STEAKS

Serves 6

2/3 cup balsamic vinegar
1/4 cup fig preserves

6 Flat Iron steaks, about 6 ounces each

5 ounces Boursin or Alouette soft spreadable cheese with garlic & herbs

Preheat grill to medium-high heat. Place steaks in one-gallon reclosable plastic bag or shallow non-metal dish.

In a small bowl or large measuring cup, mix the balsamic vinegar and fig preserves; pour over steaks and marinate 30 minutes (or up to 24 hours).

Remove steaks from marinade, discarding marinade, and season with salt and ground black pepper. Grill steaks 5-6 minutes on each side, turning once during cooking, to desired doneness or to internal temperature of 150°F -155°F. If steaks are thin (1/4" or less), reduce cooking time to about 4 minutes per side.

Remove steaks from grill, top with a spoonful of cheese and serve.

FREEZER PREPARATION: Prepare marinade as directed, and pour over steaks in one-gallon freezer bag. Seal and label.

STEAK PINWHEELS with SUN-DRIED TOMATO STUFFING

Serves 6

One 1 1/2 lb. skirt steak, tenderized

1/2 cup julienned sun-dried tomatoes (not packed in oil)
3 Tbsp. butter, melted
1 1/3 cups beef broth
2 1/4 cups stuffing mix
1/2 tsp. thyme

1/4 tsp. salt
1/4 tsp. pepper

1/4 cup beef broth

Preheat oven to 225°F. Spray a 9 x 13 baking pan with nonstick cooking spray, or line dish with foil and spray foil with cooking spray.

If necessary, prepare steak by pounding with a meat mallet to an even thickness.

In a bowl, combine the sundried tomatoes, melted butter, 1 1/3 cups beef broth, stuffing mix and thyme.

Lay skirt steak out on cutting board or sheet of waxed paper. Sprinkle with salt and pepper. Cover steak evenly with stuffing mixture. Roll up steak lengthwise, enclosing stuffing completely. Secure the seam with toothpicks. Place steak, seam side down, in the prepared pan. Pour 1/4 cup beef broth in the bottom of the pan.

Bake steak, covered, for 1 hour. Increase oven temperature to 425°F, remove cover and continue baking for 20 to 30 minutes more. Let rest for 5 to 10 minutes, then cut into 1/2" to 1" thick pinwheels.

FREEZER PREPARATION: Prepare steak roll as directed but do not bake. Cover dish tightly; label and freeze.

BEEF AND BROCCOLI STIR-FRY

Serves 6-8

3/4 lb. boneless sirloin steak, sliced thinly
1 Tbsp. olive oil
2 tsp. minced garlic
2 Tbsp. teriyaki sauce

1 tsp. ground ginger
1/4 tsp. salt
1/4 tsp. black pepper
2 tsp. cornstarch

1 Tbsp. vegetable oil
2 cups broccoli florets
1 cup broccoli slaw
2 cups sliced mushrooms
1/2 cup carrots, shredded or thinly sliced
1/2 cup red bell pepper strips
1/2 cup teriyaki sauce

4 cups cooked Jasmine rice
1/4 cup salted cashews, chopped

Place beef in one-quart reclosable plastic bag or in a shallow, non-metal dish.

In a small bowl or measuring cup, mix olive oil, minced garlic and 2 Tbsp. teriyaki sauce and pour over meat. In a separate small bowl, combine ginger, salt, black pepper and cornstarch. Set aside.

Heat 1 Tbsp. oil in a large skillet over medium-high heat. Add beef strips and seasonings; stir-fry for 2-3 minutes (increase heat if necessary). Remove beef and set aside. Add all vegetables and 1/2 cup teriyaki sauce to skillet and stir-fry for 2 minutes. Add beef back to skillet and stir-fry an additional 1-2 minutes.

Serve over Jasmine rice, and top with cashews.

FREEZER PREPARATION: Place beef strips in one-quart freezer bag. Mix marinade and pour over meat as directed. Mix spices and package in plastic deli cup or small plastic bag. Package vegetables in one-gallon freezer bag; seal. Measure 1/2 cup teriyaki sauce and package in plastic deli container or one-quart freezer bag. Seal tightly and label. Cook Jasmine rice and package in one-gallon freezer bag; seal. Package marinated beef, spices, vegetables, teriyaki sauce and rice in 2-gallon freezer bag.

SLOW COOKER FRENCH DIP

Serves 6

One 2 1/4 lb. piece of chuck roast or rump roast

1 1/2 cups water
1 1/2 cups beef broth
1/2 cup soy sauce (low sodium preferred)
2 cloves garlic, minced
2 tsp. rosemary
2 bay leaves

French rolls or sub rolls

[handwritten note:]
roast
2 cups French
onion
soup

1 can consomme
Serve with
Provolone rolls
with Boar's Huscrad sauce

Spray a slow cooker with nonstick cooking spray. Cut roast into 2" chunks and put meat in slow cooker.

Mix water, beef broth, soy sauce, garlic, rosemary and bay leaves; pour over beef in slow cooker. Cover and cook on LOW for 8 to 10 hours. After 6 hours, remove bay leaf, then use forks to shred meat (continue cooking for remaining 2-4 hours).

Serve on toasted French rolls with au jus from the cooked beef.

FREEZER PREPARATION: Cut beef into 2" chunks and package in one-gallon freezer bag; seal. Mix water, broth, soy sauce, garlic, rosemary and bay leaves; pour into one-gallon freezer bag and seal tightly. Combine both bags in another one-gallon freezer bag; seal, label and freeze.

HONEY JOES

Serves 6

1 1/2 lbs. ground beef

2 Tbsp. vegetable oil
1/3 cup chopped onion
1/3 cup chopped celery
1/3 cup shredded carrot
1/3 cup finely chopped green bell pepper

1 6-ounce can tomato paste
1 8-ounce can tomato sauce
1/4 cup honey
1 tsp. Dijon or spicy brown mustard
2/3 cup water
1 1/2 Tbsp. vinegar
1 Tbsp. Worcestershire sauce
2 1/4 tsp. chili powder
1/2 tsp. salt
1/4 tsp. black pepper

Hamburger buns

Brown ground beef in a skillet until no longer pink; drain. Wipe out skillet, then heat the vegetable oil. Add the onion, celery, carrot and chopped green pepper; saute for 3-4 minutes, or until vegetables soften. Return beef to pan, and cook mixture for 5 more minutes.

In a medium bowl, whisk together the tomato paste and remaining ingredients. Add to ground beef and vegetables; mix well and simmer, covered, for 3 to 5 minutes.

Serve on toasted hamburger buns.

FREEZER PREPARATION: Cook ground beef as directed; cool and package in one-quart freezer bag. Combine vegetable oil and vegetables in a one-quart freezer bag; seal. Mix tomato paste and remaining ingredients until well combined and package in one-quart freezer bag; seal and label. Combine all packages in a one-gallon freezer bag; label and freeze.

MEXICAN BEEF FAJITA PIZZA

Serves 6

1 cup sliced mushrooms
1/2 cup chopped green bell pepper
2 Tbsp. butter or vegetable oil

9 ounces beef fajita meat, cooked and sliced into thin strips

1/4 cup sliced ripe olives
2 cups salsa
1 cup shredded Monterey Jack cheese
1 cup shredded Cheddar cheese
3 9" prebaked pizza crusts (or larger crusts to serve 6)

In a small skillet, saute mushrooms and bell pepper in butter or vegetable oil; set aside.

Preheat oven to 400°F. Lay pizza crusts out on pizza pans or baking sheet (can line sheet with foil or parchment for easier clean-up).

Top each crust with:
>   1/3 of the sauteed vegetables
>   1/3 of the beef fajita meat
>   1 1/2 Tbsp. olives
>   3/4 cup salsa
>   1/3 cup Monterey Jack cheese
>   1/3 cup Cheddar cheese

Bake pizzas for 12-15 minutes, or until cheese is melted and toppings are heated through. Serve with shredded lettuce and sour cream, if desired.

FREEZER PREPARATION: Prepare pizzas as directed, but do not bake. Wrap tightly with plastic wrap, then with foil. Label and freeze.

TEXAS STYLE PHILLY STEAK SANDWICH

Serves 6

1 lb. beef sirloin, very thinly sliced
One loaf French bread (approximately 12" long x 4" wide); sliced lengthwise
6 ounces cream cheese, softened
1/3 cup sour cream
1/2 cup picante sauce
1 3/4 cup shredded Mozzarella or Monterey Jack cheese
1/4 cup diced jalapeno peppers, fresh or canned

Cook beef in a nonstick skillet over medium-high heat until it loses pink color. Drain if necessary.

Stir together the cream cheese and sour cream until thoroughly mixed. Spread over both pieces of French bread. Top each bread half with cooked beef pieces, picante sauce, cheese and jalapenos.

Preheat oven to 350°F. Line a cookie sheet with foil. Lay sandwich pieces on foil and bake for 10 to 15 minutes, or until cheese melts.

FREEZER PREPARATION: Prepare sandwiches as directed but do not bake. Wrap tightly in foil, then package in two-gallon freezer bag, if available. (Can also wrap sandwiches in plastic wrap, then foil to make foil easier to remove.) Label and freeze.

GOURMET BURGERS

Serves 6

2 lbs. ground round
1 Tbsp. olive oil
1/2 cup finely chopped sun-dried tomatoes
1/3 cup chopped onion
2 cloves garlic, minced
1 Tbsp. parsley flakes
1/2 tsp. salt
1/2 tsp. pepper
3 slices Monterey Jack cheese, cut into fourths

Combine ground round with olive oil, tomatoes, onion, garlic, parsley, salt and pepper. Mix thoroughly, then divide into 12 pieces. Flatten each piece into a thin patty, keeping each even in size. Lay two pieces of cheese on each of 6 patties. Top with the remaining 6 patties and seal edges well to form 6 cheese-stuffed burgers. (Be sure edges are sealed well or burgers can come apart during cooking.)

Preheat grill to medium-high heat. Grill burgers for 12 to 16 minutes, turning once. If cheese begins to leak, place a piece of foil underneath the burgers to prevent burning.

Serve on toasted buns.

FREEZER PREPARATION: Prepare burgers as directed but do not cook. Package in a baking dish, or wrap tightly in plastic wrap and place in a one-gallon freezer bag. Seal tightly and label.

MEATLOAFER BURGERS

Serves 6

3/4 cup Japanese bread crumbs (panko)
1 egg, beaten
1 Tbsp. butter
1/2 cup finely diced onions
1 clove garlic, minced
2 tbsp. dried parsley, or 1/4 cup chopped fresh parsley
1 tsp. Worcestershire sauce
1 tsp. salt
1/2 tsp. black pepper
1 1/2 ounces ground round

Tomato-Bacon Relish
3 Tbsp. chopped cooked bacon (about 2 strips)
1/2 cup finely chopped onion
1/4 cup brown sugar
1/4 cup yellow mustard
1/4 cup ketchup
1/2 cup diced tomato (seed and drain tomato before dicing)

In a small bowl, combine the Japanese bread crumbs and beaten egg; set aside. In a small skillet on the stove, or in a glass bowl in the microwave, saute the onion in 1 Tbsp. butter for 2-3 minutes or until soft.

In a large bowl, combine the breadcrumb/egg mixture, sauteed onions, garlic, parsley, Worcestershire sauce, salt, pepper and ground round. Mix thoroughly and divide into 6 pieces. Shape each piece into a burger, 1/2" to 3/4" thick.

For relish, in a small bowl, combine bacon and remaining 5 ingredients; stir well until mixed.

Grill or pan-fry burgers about 12-16 minutes, turning once, or until done. Serve on warmed buns with Tomato-Bacon Relish.

FREEZER PREPARATION: Prepare burgers as directed but do not cook. Layer in a pan, separating with waxed paper, or wrap tightly in plastic wrap, then cover with foil or package in a one-gallon freezer bag. Mix relish as directed and package in a one-quart freezer bag or plastic container with tight-fitting lid. Label all and freeze.

OUTSIDE-IN BACON CHEESEBURGERS

Serves 6

2 lbs. ground beef
1 1/2 Tbsp. Worcestershire sauce
1 1/2 Tbsp. steak seasoning (such as Montreal Steak seasoning)
6 Tbsp. shredded Cheddar cheese
2 Tbsp. crumbled cooked bacon pieces
1/2 tsp. salt
1/2 tsp. black pepper

In a large bowl, combine the ground beef, Worcestershire sauce and steak seasoning and mix well.

Divide mixture into 12 pieces. Flatten each piece into a thin patty. Top each of 6 patties with 1 Tbsp. Cheddar and 1 tsp. crumbled bacon pieces. Top each with the remaining 6 patties, then press and seal the edges (be sure to seal thoroughly, or patties will come apart during cooking).

Flatten finished patties to desired thickness and shape. Sprinkle with salt and pepper before cooking.

Grill Method: Preheat grill to medium heat. Grill burgers for 14 to 18 minutes, turning once halfway during cooking.

Pan-Fry Method: Heat skillet over high heat; add burgers and cook for 2 minutes on each side. Reduce heat to medium and cook burgers 12 to 14 minutes longer, turning occasionally.

FREEZER PREPARATION: Prepare burgers as directed. Lay in freezer dish, separating any layers with waxed paper, or wrap each burger in plastic wrap, then package together in a one-gallon freezer bag. Seal tightly and label.

JACK-O'-LANTERN CHEESEBURGER PIE

Serves 6

1 lb. ground beef
1 cup chopped onion
1 clove garlic, minced
3/4 tsp. salt
1/2 tsp. black pepper
1/4 cup ketchup
1 tsp. Worcestershire sauce
2 1/2 cups shredded Monterey Jack cheese, divided

Two 9" round pie crusts

1 Tbsp. prepared yellow mustard
1 egg
1 Tbsp. water
Orange food coloring

Preheat oven to 400°F. Line a cookie sheet with foil and spray with nonstick cooking spray.

Brown ground beef with onions in a skillet over medium-high heat until beef is no longer pink. Drain well and cool. Wipe out skillet and return beef to pan. Mix in garlic, salt, pepper, ketchup and Worcestershire sauce. Stir in 2 cups cheese. (This can be mixed in a large bowl, if desired.)

Roll out one piecrust and lay on prepared foil sheet. Brush 1 Tbsp. yellow mustard over crust. Spoon beef mixture onto the center of the crust, leaving a 2" border.

Unroll the second pie crust on a cutting board or sheet of waxed paper. Cut a Jack-O'-Lantern face into the crust. Carefully lay this crust over the beef mixture. Fold over edges and seal well.

In a small bowl, beat the egg and water. Tint with orange coloring to desired shade. Brush egg wash over top crust. Bake, uncovered, for 20 minutes. Brush again with egg wash and use remaining 1/2 cup cheese to fill eyes and mouth. Continue baking for 5 to 10 minutes.

FREEZER PREPARATION: Prepare as directed on a baking sheet or a cardboard circle, but do not bake. Orange egg wash may be prepared ahead and packaged in a plastic container with tight-fitting lid. Wrap pie tightly with plastic wrap and/or foil. Label and freeze.

SEAFOOD

ZESTY OVEN BARBECUED SHRIMP

Serves 6

1/4 cup (1/2 stick) butter

1/2 cup prepared Italian salad dressing
2 Tbsp. Worcestershire sauce
2 Tbsp. barbecue sauce
1 Tbsp. lemon-pepper seasoning
1 Tbsp. ground black pepper (leave out for milder flavor)
2 cloves garlic, chopped
2 bay leaves
2 small lemons, sliced
1 1/2 cups onion slices
2 lbs. medium shrimp (do not peel)

Preheat oven to 400°F. Place butter on a shallow roasting pan and place in oven 1 to 2 minutes, or until butter is melted.

In a medium bowl, mix together the salad dressing, Worcestershire, barbecue sauce, lemon-pepper seasoning, black pepper, garlic, bay leaves, lemon slices and onion slices.

Add shrimp to roasting pan, then pour sauce over. Stir to coat shrimp.

Bake, uncovered, for 20 minutes, or until shrimp turn pink, stirring occasionally. Discard bay leaves before serving.

FREEZER PREPARATION: Wrap butter in plastic wrap, or package in a small deli cup. Mix sauce ingredients as directed and package in a one-gallon freezer bag; seal. Package shrimp in a one-gallon freezer bag; seal. Place all bags/containers in a one-gallon freezer bag; seal, label and freeze.

PECAN CRUSTED TILAPIA

Serves 6

6 tilapia fillets, about 6 ounces each

3 Tbsp. Dijon mustard
3 Tbsp. butter, melted
1/3 cup honey

1/3 cup fresh breadcrumbs, or Japanese breadcrumbs (Panko)
1 Tbsp. dried parsley
1/3 cup finely chopped pecans
1/2 tsp. salt
1/2 tsp. black pepper

Preheat oven 375°F. Spray a baking sheet with nonstick cooking spray, or line with foil and spray foil with nonstick cooking spray.

In a small bowl, mix together the Dijon mustard, melted butter and honey. In another small bowl, combine the breadcrumbs, parsley and pecans.

Lay fish fillets on prepared baking sheet; season with salt and pepper. Brush with mustard mixture, then sprinkle over the breadcrumb mixture, pressing to adhere.

Bake fish, uncovered, for 20 to 30 minutes, or until fish flakes easily with a fork.

FREEZER PREPARATION: Prepare fillets as directed but do not bake. Lay in a single layer in a baking dish; cover tightly and freeze.

BREADED RANCH TILAPIA

Serves 6

6 tilapia fillets, about 6 ounces each

2 Tbsp. (about 1 ounce) dry Ranch dressing mix
2 1/2 Tbsp. olive oil
3/4 cup Italian seasoned breadcrumbs
1 Tbsp. melted butter

Line a shallow baking sheet or cookie sheet with foil and spray with nonstick cooking spray. Preheat oven to 350°F.

Lay tilapia fillets on prepared foil. In a small bowl, whisk together the dry Ranch dressing mix and olive oil; spread over each fish fillet. Top each fillet with breadcrumbs, then drizzle with melted butter.

Bake for 20 to 30 minutes, or until fish flakes easily with a fork. Since ovens vary, cooking time may need to be adjusted.

FREEZER PREPARATION: Prepare fillets as directed, but do not bake. Lay in a single layer in a freezer-safe dish; cover tightly, label and freeze.

HERB BAKED TILAPIA

Serves 6

6 tilapia fillets, about 6 ounces each

1/4 cup fine dry breadcrumbs
3/4 tsp. salt
1/2 tsp. paprika
1/2 tsp. onion powder
1/2 tsp. dry mustard
1/4 tsp. garlic powder
1/4 tsp. black pepper
1/4 tsp. cumin
1/4 tsp. dried basil
1/2 tsp. Italian seasoning
2 tsp. dried parsley
2 Tbsp. diced green onions

1 Tbsp. olive oil
1 Tbsp. melted butter

Preheat oven to 400°F. Spray a 9 x 13 baking pan with nonstick cooking spray, or line with foil and coat foil with cooking spray. Lay tilapia fillets in prepared pan.

In a bowl, combine breadcrumbs and next 11 ingredients. Sprinkle mixture over the fish fillets. Drizzle olive oil and melted butter over all.

Bake, uncovered, for 20-30 minutes, or until fish flakes easily with a fork.

FREEZER PREPARATION: Prepare fillets as directed, but do not bake. Cover dish tightly, label and freeze.

TILAPIA CALYPSO

Serves 4

4 tilapia fillets, about 5 to 6 ounces each

1 1/3 cups julienned white onion
1/2 cup julienned poblano pepper
1 cup julienned red bell pepper
2 cloves garlic, minced
2 Tbsp. olive oil
2 1/2 tsp. jerk seasoning
5 Tbsp. chopped fresh cilantro
5 orange slices

Preheat oven to 375°F. Line a 9 x 13 baking dish with foil and spray with nonstick cooking spray.

Saute onion, poblano pepper, red bell pepper and garlic in olive oil in a nonstick skillet over medium-high heat for 3 to 4 minutes.

Lay fish fillets in prepared baking dish. Sprinkle each fillet with 1/2 tsp. jerk seasoning, then top with 1/3 cup of the sauteed vegetable mixture, then top with 1 Tbsp. cilantro and 1 orange slice.

Bake, uncovered, for 10 to 15 minutes, or until fish flakes easily with a fork.

Fillets can also be baked in individual foil packets. Prepare each fillet with toppings as directed on a foil sheet; fold up two sides, then fold over ends to close, leaving room for steam. Bake on a cookie sheet as directed. Open very carefully after baking to allow steam to escape.

FREEZER PREPARATION: Prepare fillets, in baking dish or foil packets, as directed but do not bake. Cover baking dish tightly, or put foil packets in a one- or two-gallon freezer bag; seal, label and freeze.

TILAPIA VERA CRUZ

Serves 6

6 tilapia fillets, about 6 ounces each
3/4 tsp. ground cumin
1/2 tsp. salt
1/2 tsp. black pepper
1/4 cup chopped fresh cilantro
1/4 cup chopped green olives
1/4 cup salsa
1 14-ounce can pinto beans, drained and rinsed
2 cups diced tomatoes, fresh or canned

Cover a broiler pan with a sheet of aluminum foil; spray with nonstick cooking spray. Lay fillets on foil and season with the cumin, salt and pepper.

In a medium bowl, combine the cilantro, olives, salsa, pinto beans and tomatoes; set aside.

Turn broiler on to high. Broil fish for 3 to 5 minutes on each side, turning once. (If fish fillets are thin, check carefully while cooking and adjust cooking time if necessary.) Fish is done when it flakes easily with a fork.

Serve fillets with Vera Cruz salsa.

FREEZER PREPARATION: Lay fish fillets in a freezer-safe baking dish (line with foil for best results). Season with cumin, salt and pepper. Lay a sheet over waxed paper over fish. Mix salsa ingredients as directed and package in a one-quart freezer bag. Seal bag and lay on top of waxed paper. Cover dish tightly; label and freeze.

PARMESAN BAKED CATFISH

Serves 6

1/2 cup fine dry breadcrumbs
1/2 cup grated Parmesan cheese
1 Tbsp. paprika
1 tsp. basil

2 ounces butter, melted

6 catfish fillets (about 6 ounces each)

Preheat oven to 400°F. Spray a 9 x 13 baking pan with nonstick cooking spray, or line dish with foil and spray foil with cooking spray.

In a shallow pan, mix together the breadcrumbs, Parmesan, paprika and basil. Brush fish fillets with melted butter, then dip fish in breadcrumb mixture, turning to coat.

Lay fillets in prepared pan and bake, uncovered, for 10 to 15 minutes, or until fish flakes easily with a fork. Since oven temperatures may vary, fish may take longer to cook than directed.

FREEZER PREPARATION: Wrap fish fillets in plastic wrap (can wrap individually for quicker thawing), then package in a one-gallon freezer bag. Portion butter (not melted) in plastic wrap or small deli container. Mix together breadcrumbs and spices and package in a small plastic bag. Package all ingredients in a larger freezer bag; seal and label.

BAKED SALMON FILLET in PUFF PASTRY

Serves 4

1 sheet prepared puff pastry
1/2 lb. (8 ozs.) salmon fillet
1 tsp. Emeril's Essence seasoning
2 Tbsp. Garlic & Herb Boursin cheese
1 cup prepared saffron (yellow) rice
1/2 cup spinach, chopped, fresh or frozen (<u>well</u> drained)
1/2 cup diced tomatoes, fresh or canned, drained

1 egg
1 Tbsp. water

Preheat oven to 350° F. Prepare a 9 x 13 pan or baking sheet by spraying with nonstick cooking spray, or line with foil.

Thaw puff pastry, if frozen. Roll out until smooth and flatten any curled edges.

Cut salmon fillet in half and place on the puff pastry sheet, 1" from bottom edge, and allowing space between the salmon pieces (see diagram below). Sprinkle salmon with the Emeril's Essence, then spread 1 Tbsp. Boursin cheese onto each piece of salmon. Top each piece with half of the saffron rice, half of the spinach and half of the tomatoes.

Fold top half of the pastry over the salmon "stacks" and seal edges of the pastry by folding over and pinching together. (If edges will not seal, moisten with a small amount of water.) Cut two 1/2" steam vents in top of pastry.

Bake for 30 to 40 minutes, or until golden brown. Slice to serve.

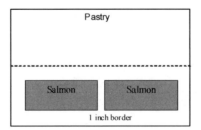

FREEZER PREPARATION: Prepare as directed above, but do not bake. Place in prepared baking pan; cover and seal tightly, label and freeze.

ORANGE KISSED SALMON and VEGETABLES

Serves 4

4 foil sheets, about 18" x 24"
4 4-ounce skinless salmon fillets
2 cups thinly sliced carrots
2 cups sliced mushrooms
1/2 cups sliced green onions
2 tsp. grated orange peel
2 tsp. dried oregano
4 cloves garlic, peeled and cut in half
1/4 tsp. salt
1/4 tsp. black pepper
4 tsp. olive oil
2 oranges, thinly sliced
4 tsp. dry white wine

Spread out foil sheets and lightly spray with cooking spray. Preheat oven to 375°F.

Divide the vegetables among the 4 pieces of foil, mounding in the center of each sheet. Place two pieces of garlic on top of vegetables. Lay 1 salmon fillet on top of each.

Drizzle 1 tsp. olive oil and 1 tsp. white wine over each piece of salmon. Season lightly with salt and pepper. Top each with orange slices.

Bring together 2 opposite edges of foil and seal with a double fold. Fold remaining ends to completely enclose the food, allowing space for steam to build.

Place packets in a single layer on a baking sheet or shallow baking pan. Bake for 40 to 45 minutes, or until carrots are tender and fish flakes easily with a fork. **Use caution when opening packets -- open slowly to allow steam to escape.**

FREEZER PREPARATION: Prepare packets as directed. Package foil packets in a single layer in a large freezer bag; seal and freeze.

ORANGE-GLAZED SALMON

Serves 4

3 Tbsp. low-sodium or no-salt-added Creole seasoning
2 tsp. brown sugar

4 6-ounce skinless salmon fillets

1 Tbsp. vegetable or olive oil

1/4 cup orange marmalade
2 Tbsp. lime juice

In a small bowl, mix the Creole seasoning and brown sugar. Sprinkle over both sides of salmon fillets.

Heat oil in a non-stick skillet over medium-high heat. Place salmon fillets in pan and saute 3 to 4 minutes; turn over and cook an additional 2 to 3 minutes.

Whisk together marmalade and lime juice, then pour into the skillet. Baste or turn fish to coat with sauce.

FREEZER PREPARATION: Combine Creole seasoning and brown sugar; package in a small plastic bag. Wrap salmon tightly in plastic wrap, then package in a one-gallon freezer bag; seal. Whisk together marmalade and lime juice and package in a plastic container with a tight-fitting lid; seal. Place all containers in a one- or two-gallon freezer bag; seal and label.

IT'S-NOT-YOUR-MOTHER'S TUNA CASSEROLE

Serves 6

8 ounces medium egg noodles, uncooked
2 tsp. butter, margarine or vegetable oil
1/2 cup each chopped onion and celery
2 Tbsp. melted butter
1/4 cup flour
2 1/4 cups milk
1 Tbsp. chicken base or 2 tsp. chicken bouillon granules
1/2 tsp. salt
1/4 tsp. black pepper
20 ounces chunk Albacore tuna, drained and flaked
1 clove garlic, minced
1/3 cup chopped mushrooms
1 cup frozen peas
1 1/2 cups shredded Cheddar cheese

1 cup crushed potato chips

Preheat oven to 350°F. Spray a 9 x 13 baking dish with nonstick cooking spray.

Cook noodles according to package directions; drain, rinse and cool. In a small skillet, saute the onion and celery in the butter for 3-4 minutes, or until softened.

In a large bowl, whisk together the 2 Tbsp. melted butter and flour. When thoroughly mixed, stir in the milk, chicken base or bouillon, salt and pepper. Stir in the sauteed onions and celery, tuna, garlic, mushrooms, peas, cheddar cheese and noodles. Top with crushed potato chips.

Bake, uncovered, for 30-35 minutes or until heated through.

FREEZER PREPARATION: Prepare casserole as directed but do not bake. Cover pan tightly, label and freeze.

SEASIDE SHORTCAKES

Serves 6

1/3 cup milk
2 cups prepared Alfredo sauce
8 ounces cream cheese, softened
1/2 tsp. dried chives (or fresh)
1 cup frozen peas
1 cup cooked salad shrimp
4 ounces crabmeat, fresh or canned

6 buttermilk biscuits, frozen, refrigerated or prepared fresh

1/2 cup shredded Cheddar cheese
1/4 cup chopped chives or chopped green onions

Using a hand mixer, mix together the milk, Alfredo sauce, cream cheese and chives until smooth. Pour mixture into a large saucepan, stir in the frozen peas, shrimp and crab meat. Heat over medium-low heat for 8 to 10 minutes, until smooth and peas are heated through, stirring occasionally.

If using pre-cooked biscuits, heat on a cookie sheet until warmed through. If using frozen or refrigerated biscuits, bake according to package directions.

To serve, split biscuits; place bottom halves on plates and spoon a serving of seafood mixture over. Cover with biscuit top, spoon more seafood mixture over the top, then sprinkle with Cheddar cheese and chives.

FREEZER PREPARATION: Mix milk, Alfredo sauce, cream cheese and chives as directed. Stir in seafood and peas. Pour mixture into a one-gallon freezer bag; seal well (double-bag if desired). Use frozen buttermilk biscuits and portion 6 biscuits in a one-quart freezer bag; seal. Portion cheddar cheese and chopped chives or onions in a small plastic bag. Place all packages in another one- or two- gallon freezer bag; seal, label and freeze.

HOT CRAB DIP

12 appetizer servings

3/4 cup sour cream
2 Tbsp. lemon juice
1 tsp. Worcestershire sauce
1 Tbsp. grated fresh onion
3/4 tsp. dry mustard
1/4 tsp. garlic powder
8 ounces cream cheese, softened
1/2 cup shredded sharp Cheddar cheese
12 ounces crab meat
1 dash paprika

Preheat oven to 325°F. Spray a 9" round or 8 x 8 baking dish with nonstick cooking spray.

In a bowl, combine the sour cream, lemon juice, Worcestershire sauce, onion, dry mustard, garlic powder and cream cheese and mix well. Stir in the Cheddar cheese and crab meat. Spoon into prepared dish and sprinkle paprika over.

Bake, uncovered, for 30 minutes or until heated through.

FREEZER PREPARATION: Prepare as directed but do not bake. Cover tightly, label and freeze.

SOUTHERN CRAB CAKES

Serves 6

1 Tbsp. mayonnaise
1 tsp. Dijon or Creole mustard
1/2 tsp. prepared horseradish
3 Tbsp. finely chopped green onion
3 Tbsp. finely diced red bell pepper
1/4 cup crushed saltine crackers
1 egg, lightly beaten
1/4 tsp. cayenne pepper
1/4 tsp. salt
1/4 tsp. black pepper
1/2 tsp. Old Bay seasoning
1 lb. lump crab meat

1/2 cup fine dry breadcrumbs

> **Handy Tip:**
>
> These crab cakes are delicious served with the Creole Sauce from Chicken Cakes with Creole Sauce (page 38).

In a bowl, mix together the mayonnaise, mustard, horseradish, green onion, red bell pepper, saltine crackers, egg, cayenne pepper, salt, black pepper and Old Bay seasoning. Gently mix in crab meat, being careful not to overmix (crab should be in large pieces). Divide mixture into 6 portions and form each into a crab cake.

Pour the breadcrumbs into a shallow pan, and lightly coat each crab cake. Refrigerate cakes until ready to cook.

In a nonstick skillet over medium-high heat, pan-fry crab cakes in a small amount of oil until browned, 4 to 6 minutes, turning once. Drain on paper towels.

FREEZER PREPARATION: Prepare crab cakes as directed but do not cook. Arrange in a freezer-safe pan in a single layer (or with waxed paper separating layers). Cover pan tightly, label and freeze.

SOUP

CHICKEN & DUMPLINGS

Serves 6

1/4 cup diced celery
1/4 cup diced onion
1 tbsp. vegetable oil or butter

5 1/2 cups chicken broth (44 ounces)
3/4 cup water
1/3 cup sour cream
1/3 cup cream of celery soup
1/3 cup cream of chicken soup
1/2 tsp. black pepper
1/2 tsp. thyme
1/4 tsp. onion powder
1 1/4 tsp. dried parsley

8 frozen Southern Style biscuits, thawed
1 lb. cooked chicken, diced or shredded

1 Tbsp. cornstarch
2 Tbsp. water

Heat oil in a large Dutch oven over medium-high heat. Saute celery and onion until tender, about 2-3 minutes. Lower heat and add broth, water, sour cream, soups and seasonings; mix well until soups and sour cream are fully incorporated. Raise heat and bring soup mixture to a boil.

Pinch off 1" pieces of biscuits and drop into boiling soup. Lower heat and simmer for 15 minutes. Gently stir in cooked chicken. In a small bowl, mix 1 Tbsp. cornstarch with 2 Tbsp. water; stir cornstarch mixture into soup, stirring gently, and cook an additional 5 minutes.

FREEZER PREPARATION: Saute onion and celery as directed, then mix together with broth, water, sour cream, soups and seasonings. Stir well and pour into 1-gallon freezer bag and seal tightly (double-bag, if desired). Put 1 lb. cooked chicken into 1-quart freezer bag and seal. Put 8 biscuits into 1-quart freezer bag and seal. Measure 1 tbsp. cornstarch into small deli container, or small plastic snack bag. Package bag of soup, bag of chicken, bag of biscuits and cornstarch together into 2-gallon freezer bag; seal and label.

VEGETABLE BEEF SOUP

Serves 6

1 lb. ground beef
1 cup chopped onion

2 cups (about 6 ounces) shredded cabbage
1 cup thinly sliced celery
1/2 cup uncooked quick-cooking barley
2 cups (about 9 ounces) frozen mixed vegetables
3 cups (about 20 ounces) canned diced tomatoes, undrained
1/2 cup tomato sauce
4 cups beef broth
2 Tbsp. Worcestershire sauce
3/4 tsp. salt
1/2 tsp. garlic powder
1/2 tsp. black pepper
1/4 tsp. dried thyme

In a large skillet, brown ground beef with onion until beef loses its pink color; drain.

In a large saucepan or Dutch oven, combine the cabbage, celery, barley, mixed vegetables, diced tomatoes, tomato sauce, beef broth, Worcestershire, salt, garlic, powder, pepper and thyme. Add the cooked ground beef. Simmer over medium heat for about 35 minutes, or until barley is done.

FREEZER PREPARATION: Cook ground beef and onion as directed; drain and cool. Package in a one-quart freezer bag; seal. Mix soup ingredients as directed and package in a one-gallon freezer bag (double-bag if desired). Put both bags together in another one- or two-gallon freezer bag; seal, label and freeze.

TORTILLA SOUP

Serves 6

1 Tbsp. vegetable oil
2 cloves garlic, minced
1 cup chopped onion
1 10-ounce can diced tomatoes with green chiles (such as Rotel)
5 cups (40 ounces) chicken broth
1 cup frozen corn
1 Tbsp. cumin
2 1/4 tsp. chili powder
2 bay leaves
1/4 tsp. cayenne pepper
2 tsp. lime juice
2 cups cooked chicken, chopped or shredded
2 Tbsp. chopped fresh cilantro
2 cups corn tortilla strips
1/2 cup shredded Monterey Jack cheese

Saute garlic and chopped onion in vegetable oil in a Dutch oven or soup pot for 2-3 minutes, or until begins to soften.

Add diced tomatoes, chicken broth, corn, cumin, chili powder, bay leaves, cayenne pepper, lime juice and cooked chicken. Bring almost to a boil, then reduce heat and simmer for 30 minutes.

While soup is cooking, bake tortilla strips on a cookie sheet at 325°F until dry and crisp but not browned.

Serve soup with tortilla strips and Monterey Jack cheese.

FREEZER PREPARATION: Saute onion and garlic as directed. Mix with other soup ingredients (except tortilla strips and cheese) and package in a one-gallon freezer bag; seal tightly, double-bagging if desired. Bake tortilla strips as directed and package in a small plastic bag. Portion cheese in a small plastic bag.

BLANCO "WHITE" CHILI

Serves 6

2 tsp. vegetable oil
1/2 cup chopped onion
1 14.5-ounce can chicken broth
1/2 cup water
1 tsp. salt
1/4 tsp. cayenne pepper
1 tsp. cumin
1 tsp. oregano
1 6-ounce can chopped green chiles
1 cup white corn, canned or frozen
3 cups (about 31 ounces) Great Northern beans, drained and rinsed
4 1/2 cups (about 1 lb.) chopped or shredded cooked chicken

1 cup (8 ounces) sour cream
1/2 cup (4 ounces) evaporated milk

In a soup pot or Dutch oven, saute the onions in the vegetable oil for about 3 minutes, or until soft. Add the chicken broth, water, salt, cayenne pepper, cumin, oregano, chopped green chiles, corn, beans and chicken. Bring to a boil; reduce heat to medium-low and simmer for 20 to 30 minutes.

In a small bowl, whisk together the sour cream and evaporated milk. Remove soup from heat and stir in sour cream mixture. Serve.

FREEZER PREPARATION: Saute onions, then mix with broth, water, seasonings, green chiles, corn, beans and chicken; package in a one-gallon freezer bag (double-bag if desired). Whisk together the sour cream and evaporated milk and package in a plastic container with a tight-fitting lid.

A-MAIZ-ING CORN CHOWDER

Serves 6 to 8

2 slices bacon, diced
1 cup chopped onion

2 cups (16 ounces) evaporated milk
1/3 cup water
1 14-ounce can cream-style corn
2 cups frozen corn
1/2 tsp. salt
1/2 tsp. black pepper
1 Tbsp. melted butter
1/2 cup instant potato flakes
2 cups frozen cooked potato cubes
1/2 cup diced ham

In a large saucepan or Dutch oven, saute the diced bacon over medium-high heat until browned. Remove bacon and drain on paper towels. Remove all but 1 to 2 tsp. bacon drippings. Saute chopped onion in bacon drippings for 3 to 4 minutes.

Add remaining ingredients to pan and simmer soup over medium heat for 15 to 20 minutes or until heated through. Stir cooked bacon in before serving.

FREEZER PREPARATION: Cook bacon as directed; drain, cool and package in a small plastic bag. Combine all other ingredients in a one-gallon freezer bag (double-bag if desired); seal tightly and label. Freeze.

TUSCAN SOUP FLORENTINE

Serves 6

1 lb. pork tenderloin or pork loin
1 Tbsp. lemon pepper seasoning
1/2 cup chopped onion
1 Tbsp. olive oil
1 14-ounce can diced tomatoes, undrained
1/2 tsp. dried basil
1/2 tsp. dried oregano
1 clove garlic, minced
5 cups chicken broth
1 15-ounce can Great Northern Beans
1/2 cup Orzo pasta, uncooked (about 3 ounces dry)
1/3 cup chopped spinach, thawed and drained if frozen

1 cup grated Parmesan cheese

Preheat oven to 350°F. Spray a 9 x 13 baking dish, or a shallow roasting pan, with nonstick cooking spray, or line the baking pan with foil and spray foil with cooking spray.

Season pork with lemon pepper seasoning. Roast pork for 30 to 45 minutes, or until pork reaches an internal temperature of 165°F. Let pork cool, then cut into 1/2" cubes.

For soup, combine pork pieces, chopped onion, olive oil, tomatoes, basil, oregano, garlic, chicken broth and beans in a large saucepan or Dutch oven. Cover and simmer over medium heat for 10 minutes. Increase heat to medium-high; add Orzo pasta and cook an additional 8 to 10 minutes or until pasta is tender. Stir in spinach and cook an additional 2 minutes.

Ladle soup into bowls and top with Parmesan cheese.

FREEZER PREPARATION: Roast pork as directed; cool and cut into 1/2" cubes. Package pork in a one-quart freezer bag; seal. Combine onion, olive oil, tomatoes, basil, oregano, garlic, chicken broth and beans in a one-gallon freezer bag; seal (double-bag if desired). Portion spinach in a small plastic bag; seal. Portion Orzo pasta in a small plastic bag; seal. Combine all bags into a two-gallon freezer bag; label and freeze.

MINI MEATBALL SOUP

Serves 6

1 lb. ground beef
1 egg
2 cloves garlic, minced
1/2 cup shredded Parmesan cheese
1/2 cup plain fine breadcrumbs

6 cups chicken broth
2 cups water
1/2 cup shredded carrots
1 cup sliced celery
1/2 cup chopped onion
2 bay leaves
1/2 tsp. salt
1/2 tsp. black pepper

1 1/2 cups dry macaroni or other small pasta
1 cup (about 9 ounces) frozen spinach, drained well and chopped

In a large bowl, combine the ground beef, egg, garlic, Parmesan and breadcrumbs. Mix throughly and form into small meatballs, about 1" in diameter. Set aside.

In a soup pot or Dutch oven, combine the chicken broth, water, carrots, celery, onion, bay leaves, salt and pepper. Bring to a boil, then reduce heat to medium. Drop meatballs, one at a time, into soup. Add pasta, cover and simmer for about 15 minutes.

Add spinach to soup and stir gently to mix in. Heat 5 to 10 more minutes or until spinach is heated.

FREEZER PREPARATION: Prepare meatballs as directed. Place in a freezer-safe dish, or lay in a one-gallon freezer bag so meatballs retain shape. Combine broth, water, carrots, celery, onion, bay leaves, salt and pepper in a one-gallon freezer bag; seal well (double-bag if desired). Portion dry pasta in a small bag; seal. Package spinach in a separate bag; seal. Combine all packages in a two-gallon freezer bag; label and freeze.

CREOLE SAUSAGE with RICE AND BEANS

Serves 6

1 lb. smoked sausage, any flavor

1 14.5-ounce can diced tomatoes, with juice
1 14-ounce can diced tomatoes with green chiles
1/2 tsp. Creole seasoning

2 cups uncooked white rice
2 14-ounce cans chicken broth

1 28-ounce can red kidney or pinto beans, rinsed and drained

Slice smoked sausage into 1/4" slices. In a large Dutch oven over medium-high heat, saute the sausage until lightly browned. Drain and return sausage to pan.

Add diced tomatoes, tomatoes with green chiles and Creole seasoning. Reduce heat to medium-low and simmer for 30 minutes. While sausage mixture is cooking, prepare the rice. In a separate pot, bring the chicken broth to boil; add the rice, reduce heat to low, cover and simmer for about 20 minutes, or until liquid is absorbed.

Stir beans into the sausage mixture and cook an additional 5 to 10 minutes. Stir in rice (may serve sausage mixture over the rice, if desired) and serve.

FREEZER PREPARATION: Slice sausage and brown as directed. Drain, cool and package in one-quart freezer bag; seal. Prepare the rice as directed and package in a one-gallon freezer bag; seal. Combine both tomatoes, Creole seasoning and beans (double bag if desired). Pour into a one-gallon freezer bag and seal tightly. Put all bags into a two-gallon freezer bag; seal and label.

JAMBALAYA

Serves 6

10 ounces jalapeno-flavored pork sausage, cut into 1/4" slices
1 1/2 cups large onion pieces
1 1/2 cups large green bell pepper pieces
1 cup sliced mushrooms
3 cloves garlic, minced
1 14.5-ounce can diced tomatoes, undrained
10 ounces small shrimp, peeled and deveined
1 cup diced cooked chicken
1 tsp. Italian seasoning
1 tsp. Tabasco sauce
1/2 tsp. garlic salt
1/2 tsp. black pepper

4 cups cooked white rice

In a large skillet, over medium-high heat, saute sausage, onion, bell pepper, mushrooms and garlic until sausage is browned and vegetables begin to get tender. Add diced tomatoes, shrimp, chicken, Italian seasoning, Tabasco, garlic salt and black pepper. Continue cooking for 3 to 5 minutes, or until shrimp turns opaque.

Serve over rice, or stir rice into Jambalaya mixture before serving.

FREEZER PREPARATION: Package sliced sausage in a one-gallon freezer bag with onion, bell pepper, garlic and mushrooms; seal. In a bowl, combine the diced tomatoes, chicken, shrimp, Italian seasoning, Tabasco, garlic salt and black pepper. Pour into a one-gallon freezer bag and seal tightly (double-bag if desired). Portion cooked rice in a separate one-gallon freezer bag. Put all bags into a two-gallon freezer bag; seal and label.

SIDE DISHES

TWO-CHEESE SQUASH CASSEROLE

Serves 8-10

4 lbs. yellow squash, sliced 1/4" thick
4 Tbsp. melted butter, divided
1 cup chopped onion
1 clove garlic, minced
2 1/2 cups coarse breadcrumbs, divided
1 1/4 shredded Parmesan cheese, divided
1 cup shredded Cheddar cheese
1/2 cup diced green onions
1/4 cup parsley
1 cup sour cream
1 tsp. salt
1 tsp. black pepper
1 egg
1/4 tsp. garlic salt

Preheat oven to 350°F. Spray a 9 x 13 baking pan with nonstick cooking spray.

Cook squash in boiling water for 8 to 10 minutes, or just until tender. Drain well (pat dry with paper towels if necessary).

Saute onion and garlic in 2 Tbsp. butter over medium heat for 3 to 4 minutes or until soft.

In a large bowl, combine the squash, sauteed onion and garlic, 1 cup breadcrumbs, 3/4 cup Parmesan, Cheddar, green onions, parsley, sour cream, salt, pepper and egg.

In a small bowl, combine the remaining 1 1/2 cups breadcrumbs, 1/2 cup Parmesan and 1/4 tsp. garlic salt. Stir in the remaining 2 Tbsp. melted butter.

Spoon squash mixture in prepared baking pan. Sprinkle breadcrumb topping over. Bake, uncovered, for 40 to 45 minutes or until heated through.

FREEZER PREPARATION: Prepare as directed but do not bake. Cover pan tightly, label and freeze.

SPICY OVEN ROASTED POTATOES

Serves 6

5 cups (about 22 ounces) frozen potato cubes, wedges, fries or fresh potatoes, cubed
1/4 cup olive oil

1 tsp. garlic powder
1 tsp. salt
2 tsp. oregano
2 tsp. basil

1 tsp. cumin
1 tsp. coriander
1/2 tsp. paprika
1/2 tsp. cayenne pepper
1/2 tsp. chili powder

Preheat oven to 375°F. Line a shallow baking sheet with foil and spray with nonstick cooking spray.

Toss the potatoes with all other ingredients in a large bowl; spread potatoes out on baking sheet. Bake for 30 to 40 minutes or until tender and golden brown.

FREEZER PREPARATION: Prepare potatoes as directed but do not bake. Package in foil pan, foil packet folded and sealed, or one-gallon freezer bag.

NOTE: Do not freeze fresh potatoes; they will turn color during the freezing process.

HONEY GLAZED CARROTS

Serves 8

5 cups thinly sliced carrots
3 Tbsp. chopped parsley
2 Tbsp. honey

1/2 tsp. salt
1/4 tsp. black pepper
1/2 tsp. grated orange rind

In a large saucepan, boil carrots in 1 1/2 quarts water until tender. Drain, return to pan and stir in remaining ingredients, adjusting seasoning to taste (can add butter if desired).

FREEZER PREPARATION: Prepare carrots as directed, cool and portion into microwaveable containers. Label and freeze.

GOURMET MASHED POTATOES

Serves 10

5 1/2 cups prepared mashed potatoes

1/4 chopped cooked bacon
1/4 cup minced onion
1/4 cup finely chopped green onions
2 cloves garlic, minced
1 cup sour cream
1/2 cup butter, melted
1 tsp. salt
1/4 tsp. black pepper
1 tsp. soy sauce

6 sheets phyllo pastry, thawed if frozen
1 Tbsp. melted butter

Preheat oven to 350°F. Spray a 9 x 13 baking dish with nonstick cooking spray.

In a large bowl, combine mashed potatoes, bacon, onion, green onions, garlic, sour cream, 1/2 cup melted butter, salt, pepper and soy sauce.

Place 2 sheets phyllo pastry on the bottom of the prepared baking dish. Cover remaining phyllo with a damp towel until ready to use. Spread one-half of the potato mixture over the pastry; add two more sheets of phyllo pastry, then top with the remaining potato mixture. Top with one phyllo pastry sheet, brush with melted butter, then cover with the last sheet of pastry.

Bake, uncovered, for 35 to 45 minutes.

FREEZER PREPARATION: Prepare as directed but do not bake. Cover dish tightly, label and freeze.

HOMESTYLE MACARONI & CHEESE

Serves 8

8 cups cooked large elbow macaroni (about 3 cups dry pasta)

2 Tbsp. melted butter
2 Tbsp. flour
1 1/4 cups (10 ounces) evaporated milk
1 1/2 cups milk
2 eggs, beaten
1/2 tsp. salt
1/2 tsp. black pepper
8 ounces shredded or cubed processed cheese (Velveeta or equivalent)
2 cups shredded Cheddar cheese
1/2 cup shredded Parmesan cheese
1/2 cup bread crumbs
1/2 cup shredded Cheddar cheese
2 Tbsp. melted butter

Preheat oven to 350°F. Spray a 9 x 13 baking pan with nonstick cooking spray. Add the cooked macaroni to the pan.

In a large bowl, whisk together the melted butter and flour, then whisk in the evaporated milk, milk, eggs, salt and pepper. Stir in the processed cheese, 2 cups Cheddar cheese and Parmesan cheese. Mix well and pour over the macaroni.

Bake, uncovered, for 40 minutes. In a small bowl, mix together the bread crumbs, 1/2 cup Cheddar cheese and melted butter. Sprinkle over the casserole then bake an additional 15 minutes. Remove from oven and let stand 10 minutes before serving.

FREEZER PREPARATION: Prepare as directed but do not add topping, and do not bake. Mix topping as directed and package in a small freezer bag. Cover baking dish tightly, label and freeze. Freeze topping bag separately.

STUFFING YOUR WAY

Serves 8 to 10

1/4 cup (1/2 stick) butter, melted
1 cup chopped celery
3/4 cup chopped onion
4 to 4 1/2 cups chicken broth
3/4 tsp. salt
1/2 tsp. poultry seasoning
1/4 tsp. black pepper
1 egg
4 cups cornbread cubes for stuffing
4 cups white bread stuffing cubes

Optional Add-Ins:
6 ounces cooked turkey, chopped
6 ounces pork sausage, cooked
1/2 cup dried cranberries
1/2 cup pecan pieces

Preheat oven to 350°F. Spray a 9 x 13 baking pan with nonstick cooking spray.

In a large bowl, combine the melted butter, celery, onion, chicken broth, salt, poultry seasoning, pepper and egg. Mix well, then stir in the dry stuffing crumbs. Stir in any Optional Add-Ins desired. Spoon stuffing into prepared pan.

Bake, covered, for 30 minutes. Remove cover and continue cooking 20 more minutes.

FREEZER PREPARATION: Prepare stuffing as directed but do not bake. Cover tightly, label and freeze.

SWEET POTATO SOUFFLE CRUNCH

Serves 6

3 cups cooked sweet potatoes, mashed (can be prepared fresh, or canned)
1/2 cup sugar
1/3 cup (about 3 ounces) butter, melted
1 tsp. vanilla extract
3/4 cup evaporated milk
2 eggs

1/2 cup flour
1 cup brown sugar
1/2 cup (1 stick) butter, melted
3/4 cup chopped pecans

Preheat oven to 350°F. Spray a 9 x 13 baking pan with nonstick cooking spray.

In a large bowl, mash the sweet potatoes. Using a hand mixer, mix in the sugar, butter, vanilla extract, evaporated milk and eggs. Pour into prepared pan.

In a small bowl, mix together the flour, brown sugar, melted butter and pecans. Sprinkle mixture over sweet potatoes in pan.

Bake, uncovered, for 30 minutes or until browned.

FREEZER PREPARATION: Prepare as directed but do not bake. Cover pan tightly; label and freeze.

DESSERTS

STRAWBERRY MARGARITA DESSERT

Serves 10

1 1/4 cups crushed pretzels
1/4 cup sugar
1/2 cup (1 stick) unsalted butter, melted

1 14-ounce can sweetened condensed milk
1/2 cup frozen margarita mix concentrate
1 1/2 cups frozen strawberries in syrup, thawed
1 cup whipped topping

For crust, mix the pretzel crumbs, sugar and melted butter and press firmly into a 9" round or 8 x 8 square pan.

With a hand mixer or whisk, mix the sweetened condensed milk and margarita mix. Stir in the strawberries, then fold in the whipped topping.

Pour filling over crust and spread evenly. Cover and freeze.

Remove from freezer and let dessert sit out at room temperature for 15 to 20 minutes before serving.

FREEZER PREPARATION: Prepare as directed; label and freeze.

GUILTLESS BROWNIES

Yields 24 pieces

1/2 cup (1 stick) margarine, softened
3/4 cup Splenda Sugar Blend for Baking
2 eggs

2 cups all-purpose flour
2 Tbsp. cocoa
1 1/2 tsp. salt
1 tsp. baking soda
1/2 tsp. ground cinnamon
2 cups applesauce
3/4 cup semisweet chocolate chips

1/4 cup chopped walnuts

Preheat oven to 350°F. Spray a 9 x 13 baking pan with nonstick cooking spray.

In a mixer bowl, beat the margarine and Splenda until creamy. Beat in the eggs until well mixed.

In a separate bowl, combine the flour, cocoa, salt, soda and cinnamon. Stir the dry ingredients into the margarine mixture alternately with the applesauce, mixing well after each addition. Stir in chocolate chips

Pour batter into prepared pan. Sprinkle walnuts over the batter.

Bake for 30 to 35 minutes, or until a toothpick inserted in the center comes out clean.

FREEZER PREPARATION: Prepare batter as directed but do not bake. Cover pan tightly, label and freeze.

CHOCOLATE DECADENCE DESSERT

Serves 10

1 1/4 cups chocolate cookie crumbs (Oreo)
3 Tbsp. sugar
1/4 cup finely chopped pecans, toasted
1/3 cup (about 3 ounces) butter, melted

1 4.2-ounce package chocolate mousse mix
1 cup milk

4 ounces cream cheese, softened
1/2 cup powdered sugar
1 3/4 cups whipped topping, divided

In a 9" round pan, mix the chocolate cookie crumbs, sugar, pecans and melted butter. Mix well and press onto the bottom of the pan.

Prepare chocolate mousse with 1 cup milk, according to package directions. In a separate mixing bowl, beat together the cream cheese, powdered sugar and 3/4 cup whipped topping. Spread over the prepared crust, then top with the chocolate mousse, smoothing evenly to the sides of the pan. Top with remaining 1 cup whipped topping.

Garnish with chocolate shavings or chocolate decorative sprinkles.

FREEZER PREPARATION: Prepare dessert as directed. Cover tightly, label and freeze.

FLOWER POT CAKE

Serves 8

1 small (about 6" diameter) new flower pot

6 ounces cream cheese, softened
1 cup powdered sugar
1 3/4 cups whipped topping
1 1/4 cups prepared chocolate pudding
1 3/4 cups chocolate cookie crumbs (Oreo), divided
2 cups crumbled chocolate cake or brownie pieces
3 gummy worms candy treats
1 silk flower with stem

Prepare flower pot by rinsing and drying well. Cut a piece of waxed paper or *Press n Seal* wrap large enough to cover the inside bottom of the pot. Press into place.

In a large mixing bowl, beat together the cream cheese, powdered sugar and whipped topping; set aside. Prepare chocolate pudding according to package directions; set aside.

In the flower pot, layer:
> 3/4 cup cookie crumbs
> Chocolate pudding
> Cream cheese mixture
> Chocolate cake or brownie pieces
> 2 gummy worms
> 1 cup cookie crumbs
> 1 gummy worm

Insert silk flower in the center.

FREEZER PREPARATION: Prepare as directed, but do not insert silk flower. Wrap the pot with plastic wrap, covering the top well. Place pot into a two-gallon freezer bag, label and freeze. Add silk flower after thawing

FOURTH of JULY BLUEBERRY DESSERT

Serves 8

1 1/2 cups graham cracker crumbs
1/3 cup sugar
1/2 cup butter or margarine, melted
6 ounces cream cheese, softened
1/3 cup powdered sugar
3 1/2 cups whipped topping, divided
1 1/2 cups (24 ounces) blueberry pie filling

In a 9 x 13 baking pan, mix together the graham cracker crumbs, sugar and melted butter and press mixture evenly across the bottom of the pan.

With a mixer, beat together the cream cheese, powdered sugar and 1 3/4 cups whipped topping. Carefully spread over the prepared crust. To make spreading easier, drop spoonfuls of mixture over the crust, then spread. Top with blueberry pie filling, then top with remaining whipped topping.

FREEZER PREPARATION: Prepare as directed. Cover dish tightly, label and freeze.

PEACH and BLUEBERRY COBBLER

Serves 8

5 cups (about 25 ounces) sliced peaches, fresh or frozen
3 cups (about 15 ounces) blueberries, fresh or frozen
2 Tbsp. cornstarch
1/4 cup brown sugar
1/4 cup white sugar
1/2 tsp. salt
1/4 tsp. cinnamon
1 Tbsp. Minute tapioca (do not use large pearl)
3 Tbsp. butter

Prepared pie crust rolled out to 10" x 12" (or enough for 2-crust pie)

Preheat oven to 400°F. Spray a 9 x 13 baking pan with nonstick cooking spray.

In a large bowl, mix together the peaches, blueberries, cornstarch, brown sugar, white sugar, salt, cinnamon and tapioca.

Pour fruit mixture into prepared pan; cut butter into 3 pieces and lay over fruit. Lay prepared crust over the top; cut 6 slits in the crust to allow steam to escape; sprinkle with more white sugar.

Bake for 45 minutes, or until crust is evenly browned. If crust begins to brown too quickly, cover with foil for about 10 minutes, then remove and continue baking as directed.

FREEZER PREPARATION: Prepare cobbler as directed but do not bake. Cover tightly, label and freeze.

APPLE-CRANBERRY STREUSEL PIE

Serves 6 to 8

4 cups Granny Smith apples, peeled, cored and sliced 1/4" thick
1/2 cup whole berry cranberry sauce
3/4 cup sugar
3 Tbsp. Minute tapioca (do not use large pearl)
1 tsp. lemon juice
1/4 tsp. cinnamon

One 9" deep dish pie crust

Streusel Topping:
1/3 cup quick-cooking oats
1/2 cup brown sugar
1/2 cup flour
3 Tbsp. melted butter

Preheat oven to 375°F.

In a large bowl, combine the apples, cranberry sauce, sugar, tapioca, lemon juice and cinnamon. Spoon apple filling into crust.

In a small bowl, combine the oats, brown sugar, flour and melted butter until combined and crumbly. Sprinkle topping over apples, pressing to adhere.

To prevent over-browning, cover edges of pie crust with strips of foil. Bake pie for 25 minutes; remove foil and continue baking for 30 minutes or until top is browned.

FREEZER PREPARATION: Prepare pie as directed but do not bake. Wrap tightly with plastic wrap, then cover with foil or package in a two-gallon freezer bag. Seal and label.

PUMPKIN PRALINE DESSERT

Serves 12

2 cups canned pumpkin
1 12-ounce can evaporated milk
3 eggs
1 cup sugar
1 tsp. cinnamon
1/2 tsp. cloves
1/4 tsp. ginger
1/4 tsp. nutmeg
1/4 tsp. salt
1 box white cake mix
3/4 cup chopped pecans
1/2 cup (1 stick) butter or margarine, melted

Preheat oven to 350°F. Spray a 9 x 13 baking pan with nonstick cooking spray.

In a large bowl, with an electric mixer, mix the pumpkin, evaporated milk, eggs, sugar, cinnamon, cloves, ginger, nutmeg and salt. Pour into prepared pan. Sprinkle dry cake mix evenly over the pumpkin batter. Sprinkle pecans evenly over cake mix. Drizzle melted butter evenly over dry mixture.

Bake, uncovered, 50 to 60 minutes or until knife inserted in center of dessert comes out clean.

FREEZER PREPARATION: Prepare dessert as directed but do not bake. Cover dish tightly; seal, label and freeze.

INDEX

INDEX

CATEGORY INDEX

Made in the USA
San Bernardino, CA
19 December 2016